Brimming with creative inspiration, how-to projects, and useful information to enrich your everyday life, Quarto Knows is a favorite destination for those pursuing their interests and passions. Visit our site and dig deeper with our books into your area of interest: Quarto Creates, Quarto Cooks, Quarto Homes, Quarto Lives, Quarto Drives, Quarto Explores, Quarto Gifts, or Quarto Kids.

First Published in 2021 by The Harvard Common Press, an imprint of The Quarto Group, 100 Cummings Center, Suite 265-D, Beverly, MA 01915, USA.
T (978) 282-9590 F (978) 283-2742 QuartoKnows.com

The Harvard Common Press titles are also available at discount for retail, wholesale, promotional, and bulk purchase. For details, contact the Special Sales Manager by email at specialsales@quarto.com or by mail at The Quarto Group, Attn: Special Sales Manager, 100 Cummings Center, Suite 265-D, Beverly, MA 01915, USA.

26 25 24 23 22 21   1 2 3 4 5

ISBN: 978-1-59233-995-2

Digital edition published in 2021
eISBN: 978-1-63159-998-9

Library of Congress Cataloging-in-Publication Data is available.

Design and Page Layout: Amy Sly
Photography: Isaac Alongi, except where noted
Food Styling: Trina Kahl

Additional photography: pages 5, 8, 12, 14, 19, 20, 26, 62, 71, and 135 courtesy of the author; pages 64 and 65, courtesy of Paul Patterson; pages 104 and 108, courtesy of Jess Pryles; page 133, Shutterstock; pages 143 and 145, courtesy of Craig Verhage; page 172 and 173 courtesy of Matt Pittman

Printed in China

BBQ
REVOLUTION

Innovative Barbecue Recipes from an All-Star Pitmaster

MITCH BENJAMIN

Meat Mitch Barbecue and Char Bar Smoked Meats & Amusements

HARVARD
COMMON
PRESS

DEDICATION

This book is dedicated to my wife, Jennifer, son, Will, and daughter,
Piper. You have supported me, encouraged me, and most of all, put up
with me! I love you all very much and thank you from the bottom of my
heart. Without you, there would be nothing to write.

This picture of my family may go back a few years, but it's my favorite. It brings me back to a day
where we worked hard as a family making great barbecue for our local food bank, Harvesters.

CONTENTS

FUNDAMENTALS OF COMPETITION BARBECUE
16

CHAR BAR SMOKED MEATS & AMUSEMENTS
68

REVOLUTIONARY BBQ: THINKING OUTSIDE THE SMOKE BOX
110

WHAT TO DO WITH YOUR 'QUE
146

SIDES, DESSERTS, AND OTHER DELIGHTS FROM THE "MITCHEN"
178

FOREWORD

I have known Mitch for more than two decades and have enjoyed plenty of meals at his house and mine. Yeah, the food is always great . . . but it's even more fun watching him cook it! It is so much fun, in fact, that I started to cook so I could be his wing man. When he needed another ABS Smoker, he talked me into buying one. It was in my backyard for a year or two and I have not seen it since—that is, unless I visit his house!

We have had a lot of adventures together. Once, at a local BBQ competition, I brought a good friend to see everything that goes on at the Meat Mitch tent. We ate so much food that the team barely had enough food left to turn in. I'll never forget my friend asking one of the team members why he wasn't diving in. It turns out that team member was a vegetarian. Without hesitation, my friend replied: "That, my friend, is the ultimate form of hobby."

A few times a year Mitch and his team would cater the Royals locker room after a game. It seemed like it was always when those damn Yankees were in town. Not only did the Royals players love Mitch's food, but the Yankees did too. (I heard it was their favorite post-game meal from around the league.) That gave me an idea. In 2012, I arranged for Mitch and his team to do pre- and post-game meals at all the All-Star Game events inside the stadium in Kansas City. You can even pull up the Home Run Derby online and watch John Kruk scarf down ribs while broadcasting the event—it was a classic!

A few years later, Mitch and I took a trip to New York City to meet the Barstool Sports team. We were serving them BBQ and having a day of fun. We had smoked all the meat at Mitch's house and flown it there with us. While we rented a place with an oven to heat it all up, I did not realize Mitch was going to try to smoke some of the food as well. Next thing I know, the smoke alarms are going off, he's throwing the door and windows open, and security was there! Ultimately, we delivered some great food to the Barstool headquarters and fed their entire crew. Everyone had a blast.

Over the years, I have learned a lot from Mitch, and you can, too. I encourage you to try these recipes. I cannot wait to make the ones I haven't tried already! There is nothing better than smoking or grilling in the backyard with a Coors Light in the summer or a glass of red wine in the winter. So, go for it, Podsy! You will have a blast just like me: it's a *BBQ Revolution!*

—George Brett, Kansas City Royal and Major League Baseball Hall-of-Famer

INTRODUCTION
THE MEAT MITCH STORY

Not long after graduating from college, I moved from Lancaster, Pennsylvania, to Kansas City to work as a sales representative for TaylorMade Golf Company. It was my dream job and all I had thought about for ages. After a year on my own, things were going great. In fact, I felt like KC should be our new home, so my fiancé, Jennifer, joined me. We soon got a dog, then bought a house, *finally* got married, and a year later started our family.

Everything we did had a huge impact on me, including our first house. We moved in next to Jim and Marge Hickey, and we could not have been more fortunate. Jim and Marge were empty nesters with kids older than me and took us in as their own. Their backyard had a pool, a big smoker, and a refrigerator filled with beer. Jim and I became fast friends and he introduced me to smoking. We smoked ribs, briskets, pork butts, chicken, pork tenderloins . . . you name it, we smoked it!

I was not afraid of cooking. Growing up, I lived in a house where my dad cooked most of my meals. I learned a lot just from watching him. By the time I got to college, I was one of the guys that would break into the fraternity kitchen late at night and make food for myself and my buddies. By the time I was an adult, I felt that cooking was in my DNA. When I laid eyes on that smoker at Jim's house, I couldn't wait to watch it get it fired up. I watched and listened and learned—then I bought one of my own.

I still remember the day I found an Oklahoma Joe's Longhorn Smoker at a local store and brought that baby home. It was game on from there, smoking and grilling everything I could. I was constantly asking questions and slowly getting better . . . and then it happened. My other next-door neighbor took me to my first American Royal World Series of Barbecue party. *Wow!* It was awesome. Hay bales, bars, dancing, DJs, bands, Daisy Duke shorts . . . I was hooked.

The next year, I wanted to enter the contest. I named my team "Meat Mitch" and suckered a few friends, including Bruce Trecek and Jamie Burrell (Jim's sons-in-law), to help me. By October, we were in business. The goal, however, was not to win, but to have an amazing party! Well, we had a rager: I mean a knock-down, drag-out, kick-ass party. Yet we somehow still managed to successfully turn in all of our meat competition categories. Once that was done, we cleaned up our competition site, loaded up our trailer, grabbed our last full keg of beer, and high-tailed it back to my house to continue the party. There was an award ceremony that evening, but in our minds, we had already "won" and our smoked meat had nothing to do with it.

About an hour later, I received a phone call from a friend asking me where I was. He told me we never should have left because Meat Mitch won third place brisket and we were the *only* team that wasn't there to take the stage for victory!

Cory Lagerstrom, Mitch Benjamin, and Jamie Burrell at the Memphis in May World BBQ Championships.

FROM ONE BIG PARTY TO A WHOLE NEW LIFE

It would have been impossible to predict everything that would happen in the next twenty years. The Meat Mitch party at the American Royal quickly grew to mythical proportions—think 2,500 people with three huge movie screens and an LA-style DJ (see YouTube). At the same time, Meat Mitch was evolving into a proper brand. Our team started to get better and better. We began entering competitions throughout the year and expanding our scope. We were making a name for ourselves.

One of the most important things I did early in my competition career was signing up to take BBQ classes from the Baron of Barbecue, Paul Kirk, as well as competition legend Rod Gray of Pellet Envy fame. I learned so much from these two Kansas City legends and from other barbecue culinary classes and continued to make new friends inside the barbecue community. It was during this time that I was messing around with making my own sauces and rubs.

Finally, loaded with our new BBQ sauce and rub, we traveled to the Wild Blue Kansas state BBQ competition in Burlington, Kansas. We used our new Whomp! Rub and Whomp! Sauce on every entry. I was extremely nervous, because we were going to find out how the certified judges felt about our new flavors. After they declared us Reserve Grand Champion, our team went and jumped in a public pool fully clothed to cool off from the 100°F (38°C) heat! It was the best day.

I continued to work on my new craft and mess with flavors, constantly trying new meats and recipes. I asked the team to travel and compete—the core always stayed together and several awesome people came and went. Ultimately, we became a fixture at the Memphis in May World Championship Barbecue Cooking Contest, where we have now competed for a decade. It is a surreal and amazing venue along the Mississippi River. We have experienced tremendous success in Memphis and consider it a home (which I cherish, as I was born in Baptist Memorial Hospital in Shelby County, Memphis, Tennessee).

MEAT MITCH TODAY

Not long after opening the Char Bar (see page 68) in Kansas City and seeing it become remarkably successful, I decided to make the leap and leave the golf industry after 20 years. I had to pursue my passion. It was time—and everyone in my life agreed and encouraged me. You will see things like #BBQLIFE and often see mention in books and on blogs about the camaraderie, loyalty, and family that is established during competition weekends when everyone is together, smoking meats and doing what we love. It's all true: every single word of it. The friends I've made through competition cooking have taken me around the country and the world, onto professional sporting fields and national TV shows, as a guest at company events, and, of course, to countless backyards cooking for family and friends.

Around the world, did I say? Like nobody's business! Through a somewhat random online connection, I was introduced to Louis and Melissa Khenane, who have since become dear friends. They invited me to Paris, France, where I spent months helping them open Rosie's Smokehouse. While I was there, I cemented a friendship with head chef Paul Patterson (page 64). Paul is originally from New Zealand and we ended up traveling there together, staying with his amazing family in Auckland and competing

Rosie's Smokehouse, Paris, France

at Meatstock (New Zealand's big BBQ event and championship). I made even more new friends with the locals, called Kiwis, and they may have even made me an honorary citizen, but I don't remember . . . We smoked meats and we drank beers and vodka. We hit the beach; fished; blew crazy, long Didgeridoo horns; drank cava; and ate our way through the country.

As wild as that sounds, you might have surprised me more if you went back in time and told me I would one day be named barbecue ambassador by none other than hall-of-fame baseball player George Brett for the 2012 Major League Baseball All-Star Game in Kansas City. The Meat Mitch team catered all three nights: from the celebrity-packed softball game to the Home Run Derby, where I was called to the field and personally served ribs to the ESPN panel on national TV, to the All-Star Game itself. We then flew to the East Coast and catered Derek Jeter's retirement party in Yankee Stadium. We also ended up back in NYC feeding the entire Barstool Sports company, where I was fortunate to meet all their personalities and participated in skits including the one-bite pizza challenge with *El Presidente*, Dave Portnoy. My Burnt Ends scored a 9.9, the highest score ever given out.

In 2020, barbecue was what got me and my family through our toughest year ever. During the worldwide pandemic, with restaurants (including mine) under all sorts of restrictions and shutdowns, I started emailing out a weekly BBQ menu. My friends and neighbors responded in droves. Soon, while much of the city was locked in their homes, word spread and many, many more invited my food in week after week. The whole experience made a major impact in my family's life. We all pitched in and we cooked and cooked and cooked. Then we pulled together to deliver door-to-door barbecue. It is my hope that we lifted spirits and created some fun and excitement—some positive memories— during a time of so much anxiety and fear.

This book contains recipes from every part of my barbecue journey, from my competition meats (starting on page 46) and hits from my restaurant (starting on page 72) to recipes from Paul Patterson in Paris (page 66) and even desserts dreamed up during the pandemic by my daughter, Piper (page 178). To me, it all represents the BBQ Revolution. You can follow the rules and compete or you can blaze your own path and get crazy creative. All that matters is that you stay true to the spirit of BBQ, putting the comradery and friendship first, along the way.

—Mitch Benjamin

Mitch Benjamin, Tom Carroll, Yankee Hall-of-Famer Mariano Rivera, and Dan Gillham at the New York Yankees locker room.

1

FUNDAMENTALS OF COMPETITION BARBECUE

Come on in! Let's have some fun as we weave our way through the competition barbecue world. We'll take a peek through what a day in the life actually looks like. It's pretty fast-paced as you can see from a typical jam-packed competition schedule (see page 21). I'll describe what competition barbecue judges look for and discuss as they judge the food they are presented. We'll then go behind the scenes so you can learn some of my techniques and recipes for each of the competition categories. It's fun, fast, and tedious—from building clamshell boxes with greens to injecting butts to scraping chicken skins!

We'll talk rubs, sauces, and flavor profiles as well. You can learn how to make the at-home versions of some of the most decorated and award-winning rubs and sauces in the country! Finally, we'll dive into the world of smokers. I'll talk about what I use, plus offer some tips on smoker options out there. (And if you've just got a kettle grill, no problem.) I'm fired up, Jimmy! Let's talk shop!

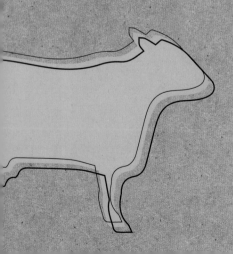

THIS IS COMPETITION BBQ

Competition barbecue is more about friendships and community than anything else. It's the sheer pleasure of meeting new people who all share the same passion. It's the pile of smoky clothes on the laundry floor and that first shower you finally take after a couple days in the heat. Personally, I love that feeling of being absolutely exhausted after a sleepless night or two of cooking and congregating. I love getting the families together for dinner afterwards, hopefully to celebrate, and then passing out early and sleeping like a baby. And I must say that there's nothing more exciting and exhilarating than hearing your name called for a category win and, if you are fortunate enough, a Grand Championship.

I could tell countless stories about my team on the biggest of competition stages, like the The American Royal World Series of Barbecue and the Memphis in May World Championship Barbecue Cooking Contest. After doing so many barbecue competitions, I often have people ask me what the days are like—and how the food is judged. While every competition is different (and heck, the same competition can be different year to year!), there are certainly enough similarities to run through a "typical" experience. So, let's jump into that right away!

THE SETUP

Traditionally, the Meat Mitch team likes to arrive around noon on Friday for weekend events. We roll in with a big trailer, complete with two or three smokers, a small grill, tents, tables, chairs, trash bags, lighting, paper towels, coolers, and every ingredient and supply we can think of (there is nothing worse than running errands instead of focusing on cooking). You might think we'd launch right into unpacking, but I find it always takes us a while once we receive our space for us to plan and figure out how we'll set it up. We try to plan as much as possible before we arrive, but sometimes we don't know if we are going to be on grass or a hard surface, if it will be flat or on an incline, and so on. Plus, there's the weather to consider. It might rain, which can change our priorities as we work to avoid the water as best as we can. Needless to say, we always struggle with the layout, and there's always a high level of satisfaction once our tents are up, tables configured, smokers in line, beer coolers made accessible, and chairs have butts in 'em.

Front row: Meat Mitch team members Jim McClymont, Mitch Benjamin, Bruce Trecek, Jamie Burrell, and Cory Lagerstrom at the Memphis in May World BBQ Championships.

One of my first tasks is to assign a team member to hunt down one of the all-powerful meat inspectors. They are generally found driving around in a golf cart, doing their best to find teams and get everyone checked in. An inspector must come into your tented area and inspect your meat coolers. But this isn't a safety or temperature check! No, the inspector is there to make sure all of the competition proteins are raw and unseasoned. (For most competitions, we bring a mix of proteins—like two pork butts, two whole briskets, sixteen chicken thighs, and six slabs of pork spare ribs). We can't season or cook ahead of time, but it *is* okay to bring pretrimmed meat to the competitions, and I highly recommend it. I strongly prefer trimming chicken and the meats at home, in my air-conditioned kitchen, as opposed to outside on a plastic table in the sun and heat. I also like to keep some of my trimming techniques to myself and to avoid people shigging from me. (*Shigging* is a barbecue term that refers to someone trying to steal your barbecue secrets by watching everything you do. But it's all in good fun, and most of us love to talk barbecue with everyone. So if you are at a competition, don't be afraid to join in the conversation.)

Sometimes teammate Bruce Trecek daydreams about what might have been . . .

Once the meat is inspected, it's time to prep the larger proteins: the pork and brisket. This is when my team adds our injections and seasons our meat, wraps it in clear plastic wrap, and gets it all cozy back in our ice coolers. Since we will have trimmed our chicken and ribs at home, they are all set in their ice coolers already. Then, we get to go on a walkabout to see our friends—beer in hand, of course! This is the best time of the competition. Catching up with old friends and making new ones is what it's all about. Most teams will always have some kind of meat rolling on a smoker, and most of us are eager for our buddies to try out our latest recipes. (I know I have had some of the best food of my life off of my friends' smokers in these hours before a competition.)

Whomp Girls Maggie Newman, Elisabeth Trecek, Molly Rapp, and Sadie Laughlin—and me in the middle.

THE COOK

By eleven o'clock on Friday night, it's time to settle down and start the fire in our smoker for the competition meats. We pull out our pork butts and briskets and allow those to rest and come to room temperature. I like to hit them with another layer of seasoning as well. At midnight, the smoker should be rolling at 225°F (107°C), and the pork butts and briskets go on. These will be on the smoker for 9 to 10 hours, and then we'll rest them in a dry cooler for several hours until we're ready to prep for our entry. At some point, while they are cooking, someone on the team will build our clamshell with the greens. (The "clamshell" or "blind box" is the stryrofoam container you serve your barbecue in.) Then, in the morning, we'll put our ribs on at 7:30 am and our chicken on at 10:30 am. (See the schedule below for a more detailed breakdown.)

MEAT MITCH COOKING SCHEDULE

	PREP	TIME ON	TIME OFF	PROCESS	TIME ON	TIME OFF	PROCESS	REST TIME	COMPLETE
Chicken		45 minutes			20 minutes				
12:00		10:30	11:15		11:15	11:35		NONE	12:00
	Whomp Rub - 10 am			Candy Sauce Boil			Grill and Baste (Whomp/ Honey) - 5 minutes		
Smart Chicken, Prep Skin	225°F (107°C)	Hickory: Apple							
Ribs		3 hours, 15 minutes			1 hour, 15 minutes		Open, drain juice.		
12:30	Trim, pull, rub (Meat Mitch Competition WHOMP! Rub)	7:30	10:45	Wrap, Parkay, and WHOMP! Rub	10:45	12:00	Naked/Honey - light sauce Top - light cayenne, sauce	NONE Grill	12:30
Whole Spares Medium	225°F (107°C)								
		Pecan: Hickory							
Butts		6 hours		Stubbs and marinade	3 hours		to 197°F (92°C), in like butter	4 hours	
1:00	Inject overnight (Butchers Butt Injection) Rub (Meat Mitch Competition WHOMP! Rub)	12:00 AM	6:00 AM	Wrap in foil - LESS	6:00 AM	9:00 AM		9:00 AM	1:00 PM
Trim fat								WHOMP!, Naked, honey and apple juice	
	225°F (107°C)	2:1 Cherry: Hickory							
Brisket		6 hours			3 hours			4 1/2 hours	
1:30		12:00 AM	6:00 AM	Mop, Rub, Foil	6:00 AM	9:00 AM	to 197°F (92°C)	9:00 AM	1:30 PM
Trim fat	Brisket injection Rub (Meat Mitch Steer Season Rub)							Light sauce on back side	
	225°F (107°C)	Cherry: Hickory							
Sausage									
2:00									
Awards									
4:00									

WHAT COMPETITION JUDGES LOOK FOR

Judging varies by competition, but let's use the Memphis in May World Championship Barbecue Cooking Contest, which has on-site judging, as one example. Since it's an MBN (Memphis Barbecue Network) event, not only do we run our food to a judging area, but we also get to greet certified judges as they enter our tent, sit down, and eat our food—yes, right in front of us! It's our job to showcase our entry, embellishing the meat to bring out the gentle flavors of smoke and heat we used to bring that meat to its most tender, succulent moment. After the judges have sampled, we thank them profusely for spending time with us and judging our food. As soon as the team finishes clapping for the departing judge, we quickly clean up and get ready for the next judge to arrive. This happens three times over forty-five minutes. It is one of the most exciting and nerve-racking dog-and-pony shows I have ever been a part of, and I love it!

For the actual judging, I am going to switch gears from Memphis to my home state of Kansas where the KCBS (Kansas City Barbecue Society) events have only blind judging and a table of six judges who are given a tray of entries. Each of the six judges awards each meat entry a separate score (from 1 to 9) in three areas: appearance, tenderness, and taste.

Experienced KCBS-certified judges know what they are looking for by their formal training, yet each brings a unique palate to the event—meaning you can't predict each judge's personal tastes. I've found truth in the saying that everyone eats with their eyes first, plus at KCBS, you are judged on appearance, so it's extremely important for the food to visually jump out of the box and get the judges drooling before they taste it. As for texture and taste, here are the criteria for the key meats:

- In the chicken category, the thigh is most often turned in for judging. It's easier to keep moist and doesn't dry out as quickly as breasts. Obviously, the judges want a moist and tender chew packed with flavor, but the key element here is delivering bite-through skin; the last thing they want is a big fatty piece of skin completely coming along with their bite. With a great bite, they can look back down at the thigh and see a perfect bite mark with the crispy skin still perfectly intact (to learn how to do this, see page 55). When you accomplish that perfect bite, you get a good score!

- When it comes to pork ribs, competitors choose between St. Louis–style spare ribs and baby back pork ribs. Judges' preferences seem to vary by competition. I found out quickly in Memphis that they only want baby backs, but in KCBS events, spare ribs generally rule supreme. No matter the type, judges are looking to make sure you don't undercook or overcook your ribs. In the backyard, falling-off-the-bone ribs are revered as the best, often accompanied by back slappin' congratulations to the pitmaster. However, in competition, that style of ribs is considered overcooked—because anyone can do that! As with chicken, judges want to see a perfect half-moon bite mark left in the rib, and they want the meat to melt in their mouths—not fall to the ground. Conversely, if there is too much of a tug to pull the meat off the bone, you lose points in tenderness. (For more on ribs, see page 46.)

- The pork category is unique in that the pork butt can be presented and displayed in many different ways. I believe judges want to see versatility so I usually show pulled pork, sliced pork, and pulled chunks. One thing the judges are always looking for is a nice balance of sauce—not too much and not too little. You need to find the perfect combination for your meat through trial and error.

- The brisket category is often thought of as the most difficult. Depending on your style of cooking, hot and fast or low and slow, it may take the longest cook time. Either way, there's a very short window to make sure that you nail the tenderness. Judges want to pick up a slice and be able to pull it in half with a gentle tug. If they give it a hard tug and it doesn't pull apart, you are done. Or, if they pick up the slice and half of it falls apart, that's not good for your score, either. Nailing the tenderness is key in brisket, as is presenting melt-in-the-mouth burnt ends.

THE ALL-IMPORTANT GREENS

One of the most tedious aspects of KCBS competition barbecue is the construction of the clamshell, which is the styrofoam container in which you place the meat to be judged. Although technically optional, you really have to make a beautiful bed of greens for your meaty masterpiece. Oftentimes, this bed is constructed late—late at night after several liquid refreshments have been consumed—and generally it's completed by someone on your team who lost a bet.

It's time-consuming, and there are rules as to what you can include. Competitors may use only a mix of the following ingredients: green leaf lettuce, curly parsley, flat-leaf parsley, curly green kale, and cilantro. Everyone has their favorites; however, I still believe in the old-school parsley box. We start by tearing up loose leaves of the green leaf lettuce and establish a base. Then, we pick the tightest stems of parsley, the ones that look like mini trees, and carefully pack them together until we have built what looks like a perfect putting green. We cover the greens with a moist paper towel, and then we refrigerate them until needed, which will be overnight.

UNDERSTANDING INJECTIONS

In a competition, a judge may take only one bite, so you better make it count by packing it with flavor—that's what I mean when I say "WHOMP!" Competitors will go to great lengths to achieve that wow factor. Sauces, rubs, and brines are all common flavor-enhancing techniques—and likely ones you've used at home. But another way many teams, including

mine, add flavor, is by injecting the proteins with a liquid that contains phosphates. This creates a deeper flavor (pun intended) and also helps keep the meats incredibly moist because phosphates improve water binding, texture, and flavor stability. Using them is as simple as buying the powder—often just labeled "pork injection" or "beef injection"—mixing it with water as the package recommends, loading up a syringe or injector, and injecting the meat. Each brand and package of meat injections will have different mixing directions. Follow those. Syringes come in all shapes and sizes and at all different price points. We use a cheap one that we buy for under $10; it is plastic with a metal needle. These syringes can be found online or in most barbecue specialty stores and often in hardware stores carrying barbecue equipment. They can be used multiple times; it's just important to make sure to clean them after every use. There are a few particular brands of commercial injections that I rely on. My go-to injections come from Meat Church BBQ, Butcher BBQ, Big Poppa Smokers, and Kosmo's Q. (See Resources, page 202, for details.)

For the pork, I recommend haphazardly puncturing and shooting up the entire butt, trying to cover it all, but the *money muscle* is especially important because it makes you the money when you win! It's the section of the pork butt on the end opposite of the bone. It's a cylinder of meat about 3 inches (7.5 cm) thick that is generally carved out and sliced into ¼ inch (6 mm)-thick pieces and fanned out like a flower in your winning pork box. For the brisket, I recommend carefully creating a 1-inch (2.5 cm) grid and systematically injecting the entire brisket: flat and point.

Note that I use these injections for competitions *only*. You won't find my restaurant (or many other restaurants) using them and seldom is a backyard cookout going to be pumped up with injections. In competition, we want that one flavor-packed bite, but when you are sitting down for an entire meal, the injections make the meat too strongly flavored. (In fact, for our competition prep, we only inject the pork butt and the brisket, though some teams inject chicken and ribs, too.)

BRINES

Brines, both wet and dry, are also used to add flavor and moisture to meats before smoking. The most important ingredient in brines and rubs is the salt, with sugar or another sweetener added to balance the saltiness. Herbs and spices are usually part of the brine, for added flavor. The difference between a wet brine and a dry brine, or rub, is the added liquid in a brine, which can be water, juice, or broth. We use a wet brine with poultry and fish because they are relatively lean and need the added moisture to stay moist during the long, slow cook. We also like to pool flavored liquids around our pork and brisket when we wrap them in foil and finish cooking them during competition.

Dry brines, or rubs, are seasonings with salt as the main ingredient. Although the salt does penetrate into the meat, what rubs do is help form a crust, or bark, on the meat, which helps the smoke adhere and add flavor. We use dry rubs on pork, beef, and chicken.

MY COMPETITION RUBS AND SAUCES

When you walk into any barbecue competition tent, you'll find a sea of rubs and sauces. We like to tinker, try different combinations, mix this with that and then add a touch more of that! We all have our secrets for flavor profiles we think everyone will love. Meat Mitch has taken this a step further, and we bottle and sell our sauces and rubs all over the world. Here are home versions of some of the most decorated and award-winning sauces and rubs today. (When you hit the rest of the recipes, you'll see that you have the choice of buying a rub or sauce or whipping up a batch of your own.)

MEAT MITCH COMPETITION WHOMP! RUB

My teammate Bruce Trecek and I took a spice class years ago and put together this winning recipe. Lightening truly struck as this exact recipe is known today as our Meat Mitch Competition WHOMP! Rub and is sold throughout the world.

1 cup (200 g) sugar

½ cup (96 g) seasoned salt

½ cup (125 g) garlic salt

¼ cup (30 g) chili powder

2 tablespoons (12 g) coarsely ground black pepper

½ cup (56 g) sweet paprika

1 teaspoon ground cinnamon

1 teaspoon ground cumin

1 teaspoon ground cayenne

1 teaspoon dried marjoram

Mix all the ingredients in a large bowl until well combined. Using a funnel, pour the contents into a plastic shaker and cover with plastic wrap until you are ready to use it. Store in an airtight container at room temperature for up to a month.

TIP: You can go to MeatMitch.com and order the commercial version of this rub if you'd rather.

Makes about 3 cups (576 g) (enough to season 8 pounds [3.6 kg] of meat)

MEAT MITCH ALL-PURPOSE RUB

This is a nice compliment to the WHOMP rub that dazzles your taste buds.

1½ cups (336 g) kosher salt

¼ cup (50 g) granulated sugar

¼ cup (60 g) packed light brown sugar

⅔ cup (75 g) sweet paprika

¼ cup (30 g) chili powder

2 teaspoons ground cayenne

½ teaspoon ground turmeric

¼ cup (24 g) plus 2 tablespoons (12 g) freshly ground black pepper

¼ cup (40 g) plus 2 tablespoons (20 g) granulated garlic

2½ teaspoons (6 g) granulated onion

½ teaspoon celery seeds

½ teaspoon dried marjoram

Mix all the ingredients in a large bowl until well combined. Using a funnel, pour the spice mix into a plastic shaker and cover with plastic wrap until you are ready to use it. Store at room temperature for up to a month.

Makes about 3¾ cups (720 g) (enough to season 10 pounds [4.6 kg] of meat)

CHAR BAR TABLE SAUCE

This is the house barbecue sauce that I developed for Kansas City's famous Char Bar. It's a classic Kansas City–style sauce that has the perfect balance of sweetness, tang, and spice. When I'm looking for an everyday sauce, I want something not too rich, not too heavy, and not necessarily a competition sauce. It needs to work on absolutely everything, including your mother-in-law. This is it. My buddy Big Shommy Love said if he spilled it on the table, he would eat the table. While this recipe makes a large batch, that's the only way to make sauce. You can use the leftovers as a springboard to doctor up your own blend. Try adding peach or apricot preserves or add a splash of whiskey for a summer pork glaze.

4 cups (960 g) ketchup (I recommend Heinz)

½ cup (100 g) granulated sugar

¼ cup (60 g) packed light brown sugar

1 tablespoon (6.5 g) celery seeds

1 tablespoon (7 g) ground cumin

1 tablespoon (9 g) garlic powder

1 tablespoon (5 g) ground red pepper

1½ teaspoons chili powder

¾ cup (175 ml) apple cider vinegar

¾ teaspoon liquid smoke

½ teaspoon fresh lemon juice

1½ teaspoons coarsely ground black pepper

1 tablespoon (14 g) kosher salt

In a large mixing bowl, combine all the ingredients. Using a wire whisk, thoroughly mix, making sure there are no clumps. Transfer to a stockpot. Cook over medium heat and continue to stir until the sauce starts to make gurgling sounds and you see little volcanic eruptions. Remove the pot from the heat and allow it to cool. Store the sauce in mason jars or plastic containers and refrigerate until you are ready to use it. The sauce will keep in the refrigerator for up to 3 months, if you don't eat it all first! Heat it or at least bring to room temperature before serving for best results.

Makes 7 cups (1.6 L) of pure Kansas City, or enough to get you through a Chiefs noon kickoff tailgate party!

CANDY SAUCE

Unlike the other recipes in this section, Candy Sauce is a recipe that has been passed around barbecue competitions for decades. We have used our take on this sauce on our chicken wings to win several contests, and we use it on our competition chicken thighs. I also love it on pork belly. It's a great mix of heat and sweet; it's got some fire and still caramelizes well on your poultry.

2 pounds (900 g) light brown sugar

2 quarts (1.9 L) beef stock

2 quarts (1.9 L) Char Bar Table Sauce (see above)

1 bottle (20 ounces, or 570 ml) Tiger Sauce

10 ounces (280 g) honey (about 14 tablespoons)

1¼ cups (250 g) white vinegar

In a large mixing bowl, combine all the ingredients. Using a wire whisk, thoroughly mix, making sure there are no clumps. Transfer to a stockpot. Cook over medium heat and continue to stir until the sauce starts to make gurgling sounds and you see little volcanic eruptions. Remove the pot from the heat and allow it to cool. Refrigerate for up to 3 months in mason jars or plastic containers until you are ready to use it. Heat it up or at least bring it to room temperature before serving.

Makes 1¼ gallons (5 L) of sauce

MEAT MITCH STEER SEASON RUB

Here's some bold seasoning, with a heavy focus on pepper and a minimum of the sweet notes, that's designed specifically for beef. Meat Mitch Steer Season Rub packs a punch. In fact, it became a world champion as it was all over our first place beef short ribs at the Memphis in May World Championship Barbecue Cooking Contest.

Mix all the ingredients in a large bowl until well combined. Using a funnel, pour the spice mix into a plastic shaker and cover with plastic wrap until you are ready to use it. Store in an airtight container at room temperature for up to a month.

TIP: You can go to MeatMitch.com and order the commercial version of this rub.

Makes about 6 cups (1.2 kg) (enough to season 15 pounds [6.8 kg] of meat)

2¼ (504 g) cups kosher salt

¾ cup (150 g) granulated sugar

½ cup (60 g) plus 2 tablespoons (30 g) packed light brown sugar

3 tablespoons (21 g) sweet paprika

1¼ cups (150 g) chili powder

2¼ teaspoons ground cayenne

¾ teaspoon ground turmeric

½ cup (48 g) plus 2 tablespoons (12 g) freshly ground black pepper

2 tablespoons (18 g) garlic powder

4 teaspoons (10 g) onion powder

¼ teaspoon celery seeds

¼ teaspoon dried oregano

MEAT MITCH COMPETITION WHOMP! BBQ SAUCE

This is my first-born, my baby, a perfect Kansas City sauce. She's sweet with heat, Podsy! Sometimes, we cut it with apple juice to thin it out, and we add a touch of honey to increase the shine. It's beautiful on pork, ribs, and chicken. We have fans who put it on their eggs and their burgers. This sauce put us on the map and will make you the hero of your neighborhood! For best results, serve the sauce heated or at least at room temperature.

4 cups (960 g) ketchup
(I recommend Heinz)

4 cups (900 g) packed light brown sugar

1 cup (200 g) white sugar

2 cups (475 ml) apple cider vinegar

2 teaspoons Worcestershire sauce

4 teaspoons (16 g) Meat Mitch Competition WHOMP! Rub, store-bought or homemade (see page 28)

1 teaspoon ground cayenne

1 teaspoon coarsely ground black pepper

1 teaspoon liquid smoke

In a large mixing bowl, combine all the ingredients. Using a wire whisk, thoroughly mix, making sure there are no clumps. Transfer to a stockpot. Cook over medium heat and continue to stir until the sauce starts to make gurgling sounds and you see little volcanic eruptions. Remove the pot from the heat and allow it to cool. Transfer to mason jars or plastic containers and store at room temperature for up to a month.

TIP: You can go to MeatMitch.com and order the commercial version of this sauce.

Makes about 10 cups (2.8 kg)

YO, PODS!

Say what? Since I say it a lot and it's all over my Meat Mitch products, I've been asked over and over again what does "Pods" mean? When I moved from the East Coast to Kansas City, I was greeted with "Nice to meet ya, pards," which is short for "partner" (say it, *Pahtnah*!). I threw some East Coast flair into it and responded with a "YO, PODS!" It's just my way of saying nice to meet you, Podsy!

THE SMOKING SECTION

Early on in my competition career, I became good buddies with the guys at an upstart smoker company called American Barbecue Systems, out of Olathe, Kansas. They soon began sponsoring me, and I was able to help them by providing some detailed advice on their first unit. They have come a long way and now manufacture one of the nicest units, not only for competition, but also perfect for the backyard.

The unit I use is called the Pit Boss, and it is an offset rotisserie smoker with a firebox in the back. It burns charcoal and wood and holds temperature extremely well. The unit is very mobile, and I have three of them on my back patio. (Yes, my wife allows that!) We have six altogether as a team; the newest one is equipped with a pellet feeding system, which has gained in popularity for its ease of use and functionality.

Because it's the type I have always used, I definitely recommend a unit with an offset smoker if you're looking into buying a smoker. In an offset smoker, the food smokes in a long horizontal chamber while charcoal and wood burn in a firebox attached to one side. They aren't cheap, but they fit my style of smoking, which utilizes both charcoal and hardwoods. There's nothing wrong with vertical smokers though, if that's what you've got. Just make sure your smoker is made of a heavy-gauge metal. You'll know when you lift the lid. If it's too light, it won't hold the heat very well. The flimsy stuff from the hardware store summer sale doesn't cut it—you need walls that are at least ¼-inch (6 mm) thick.

If you haven't already bought a smoker, here's my recommendation: Start with a kettle grill, like a Weber. With one of these grills, you can grill a steak or smoke a butt—you name it. If you try smoking on one and enjoy it, then start shopping for an offset that fits your budget. (No one ever said barbecue is a cheap addiction.) But if you find you just don't have the time to smoke as much as you thought, or you don't get enough satisfaction from the kettle grill experience, you've saved yourself hundreds (or thousands!) of dollars.

PELLET SMOKERS

"Set it and forget it" is the common motto of pellet smokers. They are as easy as turning them on and dialing in your temperature (you can often do this on an app), and it will do the rest of the work for you as it slowly feeds wood pellets nonstop into the fire. Your work is done! There is a faction in the barbecue community that deems this cheating because it circumvents the efforts of the pitmaster and takes some of the art and skill away from barbecue. I agree that it's a lot more work to slave over a burning fire, constantly adding more charcoal and wood chunks while working to keep a consistent temperature. However, I still think pellets can't quite replicate the hard work of a pitmaster. In my opinion, the trade-off is that the food tastes better with live coals and wood as opposed to just the pellets. Some people will argue the smoke ring isn't as significant with pellet smoking either. (You all know how we measure ourselves? It's by the size of our ring!)

That said, pellet smokers keep getting better and better. The most popular pellet units at the time of writing come from Traeger Grills: the Timberline 850 and 1300 models and the Ironwood 650 and 885 models. The numbers signify the inches of cook space, and the Timberline is the higher-end, fully insulated model. Traeger has helped champion the popularity of backyard barbecue, and I give them immense credit for growing the barbecue business in general.

BARBECUE TOOLS AND SUPPLIES

Besides the smoker, you'll need lots of other things. This is not a comprehensive list, but these are the must-have items and tools that I have strong opinions about.

- **CHARCOAL:** I recommend lump charcoal over briquettes because I believe they burn longer and more consistently. I always use Royal Oak Hardwood Lump Charcoal.

- **WOODS:** I use pecan, cherry, hickory, and apple woods. I like to mix them and use them for all proteins. They can be found at barbecue specialty stores and hardware stores. My favorite brand is Chigger Creek Wood Products (chiggercreek.com), which can be found online. I generally use two baseball-sized chunks every 30 minutes.

- **THERMOMETERS:** I think an instant-read thermometer is a must, and a Classic Thermapen by ThermoWorks is one of the best. You should also spring for a digital probe thermometer with Bluetooth that will work with your cellphone (wireless ones require Wi-Fi). This can free up time and allow you to accomplish other things knowing that you are on track with your cook.

- **HEATPROOF GLOVES:** Don't be like me and practically lose your fingerprints after a few years of smoking. Get a good pair.

- **LIGHTER-WEIGHT GLOVES:** You'll need gloves for tasks that involve meat that's hot but when you don't need the protection of the heat-proof gloves. You can go with latex or vinyl gloves and cheap hardware store gloves. I'm allergic to latex so I go for vinyl. But whichever you buy, try this: put on white cotton hardware store gloves and cover them with the vinyl gloves.

- **FOIL PANS, FOIL WRAP, AND SO ON:** Buy extra-strength everything, even foil, because you don't want rips or tears or anything bad happening once the precious meat is inside.

- **CUTTING BOARDS:** You'll want plenty of these, including disposable cutting boards. It might sound weird, but they are pretty great when you're cooking anywhere but home.

- **KNIVES:** Sharp knives are imperative! My go-to knives are made by Victorinox. They are consistent and very reasonably priced. I also have a Shun Classic 12-inch (30 cm) Brisket Knife that is beautiful, and I like to pull that out when I am showing off (lol).

OFFSET SMOKER GUIDELINES

Let's talk about offset smokers. These guys are the real deal, a favorite among backyard enthusiasts, though they take some real skill to master.

I've heard that this style is based off the design of old-school brick barbecue pits from the Deep South where the fire is built in a box that is on one side and the smoke and heat cross the food in the bigger pit where all the meats are hanging out. Check out Rodney Scott of Rodney Scott's Whole Hog BBQ in Charleston, South Carolina (rodneyscottsbbq.com), and you can see where some inspiration comes from. The offset style has also seen a resurgence due to the work of great pitmasters such as Aaron Franklin of Franklin BBQ in Austin, Texas (franklinbbq.com).

Most "horizontal" offset smokers have a lidded barrel-shaped or box-shaped smoking area with a firebox connected to one end and positioned slightly lower. You'll usually find a chimney coming out of the larger box, with the idea being that heat rises. As you burn your fire on the low side, the heat and smoke find their way to the larger box above and out the chimney.

Controlling the heat and smoke is a real test of craftsmanship, but you can do it! The key to controlling the heat and smoke in an offset smoker is to *really* pay attention to how the air gets in the fire box and how the air pumps out of your chimney. Just remember: Fire needs air to do its thing, so open up the vents to the fire box to get the fire hotter—or close them to cool things down.

In addition to tending to the fire, you'll also likely need to rotate the food or otherwise manage the airflow to avoid uneven cooking. The temperatures in the offset smoker will be hotter the closer it gets to the fire box, so be careful! This isn't a set-it-and-forget-it kind of cooker. Get to know your smoker. You'll learn where your hot spots are and how to massage your meats through a successful cook.

READY TO START SMOKING? DO YOU HAVE EVERYTHING YOU NEED?

- Offset smoker

- 7-quart (6.6 L) chimney starter

- 1 or more 15-pound (6.8 kg) bags of charcoal (I prefer Royal Oak.) **NOTE:** Plan to go through about one bag of charcoal for every two hours of smoking.

- Fire starters: I prefer to use tumbleweed fire starters, but you can use your preferred fire starter method (like scrunched up newspaper)—but no lighter fluid! Lighter fluid is one of the biggest mistakes in BBQ. No one wants that unpleasant taste on their food. Here's a tip: You can buy Tumbleweed Natural Fire Starters online from Royal Oak; they are made from natural wood and wax.

- Hardwood chunks to fuel the fire: I always use pecan, though for a few specific meats I might add other woods into the mix along with pecan. I figure I'll use 4 chunks per hour.

- Wireless or Bluetooth probe thermometer

HERE ARE THE STEPS FOR USING YOUR OFFSET SMOKER:

1. *Completely* open up the air intake vents. Open up the chimney all the way too.

2. Get your charcoal fired up in a chimney starter using your favorite fire starter. *Remember to never use lighter fluid.* Let the charcoal burn until you see them to turn grey; then they are ready to dump.

3. Put two or three handfuls of unlit charcoal at the bottom of the firebox. Carefully spread the hot coals from the chimney over the charcoal base. I tend to herd the coals all along the back of the box, farther away from the meat, in a uniform line. This way, I feel I can keep my temperature more consistent than having coals burning all over the place.

4. Close the lid to preheat the smoker to the desired temperature. This is a critical stage. Try not to mess with it too much.

5. When you get to your desired temperature, usually 225 to 250°F (107 to 120°C) for low and slow cooking, shut the vents so they are about half closed. This should slow down the airflow, insulate the fire, and help hold the temperature. Play with the settings as every smoker is different.

6. If it's not heating fast enough, be patient. If you need to speed things up, you can spread the coal a little to increase heat or you can add additional coals, or both. The temperature always goes down after adding fresh coals, so don't be fooled; once they start burning, your temps can skyrocket.

   Once you have achieved your desired cooking temperature, add 2 or 3 wood chunks and watch some smoke roll. Tip: I don't use a lot of wood at once. I prefer to be consistent with it through the cook, adding 2 to 3 baseball-size chunks every 30 minutes until they burn through. You'll start to see the smoke in the beginning, but ideally you want a clean, clear smoke—you don't want huge billowing freight-train smoke.

7. Open the lid to the larger box and put your seasoned meats on the grates, with the larger cuts closest to the fire box.

8. Now's the part where you really cook, but don't mess with it too much. Remember if you're lookin', you ain't cookin! You need to be watching your temperature gauge (and adjust the vents accordingly), not the meat. Remember, closing the vents will decrease heat and opening them will increase heat. Add more wood chunks and charcoal as they burn through.

9. All that's left now is to follow your guidelines for each cut of meat or recipe and keep an eye on the smoker. And don't forget to have a beer!

KETTLE GRILL SMOKING GUIDELINES

One of my all-time favorite things to cook on is the Weber Kettle Grill. It's as American as baseball, Meat Mitch, and apple pie. Everyone should own a Weber grill at some point in their life. It's really the best for backyard barbecuing. They are great all-purpose cookers that can grill a mean burger and hot dog and are perfect for fish and veggies as well.

Weber grills aren't the only kettle grills on the market. Big Green Eggs and Kamado Joe are more airtight with larger basins and are excellent cookers as well.

While you don't see a lot of Weber Kettle Grills in BBQ competitions, you can do some pretty amazing things on these suckers. They are actually really great for small batches of barbecue. For just one brisket or butt, or a couple slabs of ribs, don't knock the kettle until you try it.

Kettles are the most popular charcoal grills sold, so even if you have a smoker, you may want to know how to work your way around one. The secret password here is *indirect heat*. You don't have a ton of space on a kettle, generally about 22 inches (55 cm) of total surface cooking space. The key is to build a fire and then move all of the coals to one side of the kettle. You'll put your meat on the side with no heat below it, which will allow everything to cook low and slow.

The other secret weapon for kettle grill smoking is the water pan. Go to any grocery store and you can find disposable aluminum pans in the cookware section. Get a bunch of them, Pods, they go quick! They're also great for scooping out ashes after the party is over. The water in the pan is important because it helps stave off some of the very high heat, and it creates steam to add moisture to the kettle. This makes for a nice sauna-like environment and is helpful for cooking these small batches.

Controlling the heat is another challenge here with so little space to cook on. Lots of manufacturers sell heat deflectors, which are pieces of metal that really segregate the direct heat and protect the important meats from getting burned.

At the end of the day, understanding how to control the heat and smoke in a kettle grill is just like how you do it in an offset smoker. You need to watch your vents because fire feeds on air. Rotating your meats is also critical on a kettle, or you can get a little crispy on one side and have an uneven cook.

YOU WILL NEED:

- Kettle grill with thermometer

- Chimney starter

- 1 or more 15-pound (6.8 kg) bags of charcoal (I prefer Royal Oak.) **NOTE:** Plan to go through about one bag of charcoal for every two hours of smoking.

- Fire starter (I use a Tumbleweed Natural Fire Starter from Royal Oak, but you can use your preferred fire starter . . . but no lighter fluid!)

- Disposable aluminum pan (I use the "half pan" size, which is 12 by 10 inches [30 by 25.5 cm], or the equivalent.)

- Hardwood chunks to fuel the fire (I always use pecan, although for a few specific meats, I might add other woods into the mix along with the pecan.)

- Wireless or Bluetooth digital probe thermometer for the meat

LET'S GET YOUR KETTLE GOING TO MAKE SOME NICE SMOKED MEATS.

1. Begin by filling a chimney starter about one-third full with natural lump charcoal.

2. Remove the lid from the kettle along with the grate and pile up additional charcoal on one edge of the kettle.

3. Light the charcoal in the chimney starter with tumbleweed or your preferred starter (anything but lighter fluid!). When the lit charcoal is grey and very hot, carefully pour them over the unlit charcoal. (Watch your thumbs!)

4. Place the disposable aluminum half pan on the other side. Fill it up with about a quart (946 ml) of water.

5. Cover the grill and let the temperature get between 225 and 250°F (107 and 120°C), as measured by the gauge on the lid, for real low and slow cooking, making sure to open and close the vents on the side of the fire to control the heat.

6. Add 2 to 3 wood chunks to the charcoal and place the grate back on.

7. Set your food on top of the grate above the water pan and follow your recipe guidelines. Monitor the heat inside the kettle with the thermometer gauge. Open and close the vents to add or restrict airflow, which will control the temperature.

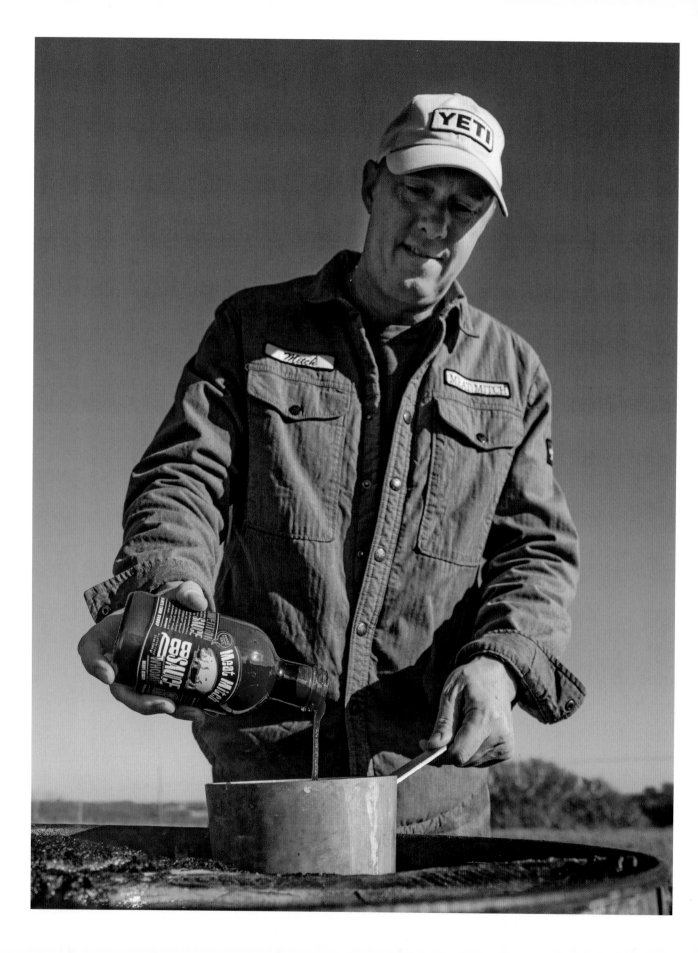

MEAT MITCH TIPS
FOR BACKYARD SMOKING

- Use your senses. Channel Stevie Wonder if you want to cook better brisket. When he's playing music, he's not looking at anything—he's feeling and listening. Do the same thing when you cook! Smell, listen, taste . . . singing is optional but encouraged!

- Barbecue is community. You probably have neighbors who can't wait to help you by sharing their experience. No neighbors that smoke? Go online! Look for groups, forums, videos, you name it. Never before has this much great information been out there on social media (just be leery of the comments . . . you never know who's been drinking!).

- Learn from the best. Take classes from pros if they are offered in your area. They can be spendy, but the good ones are well worth it.

- Patience is a virtue. If you ask me if it's done, I'm probably gonna tell you no. You need patience!

- Don't listen to everyone. If it tastes good to you and most people around you, don't get bummed out by one or two critics. But keep an open mind! There's always room to learn.

- It's okay to be cheap. Learn on the cheap meats, but not from the cheap seats. Dive in there, Podsy, and get after it. Buy a pork butt; it's by far one of the most forgiving and tasty proteins out there. When you make mistakes, you are actually making progress.

- Take it easy. Try to get some easy wins by starting off with easier things to smoke. Try not to get over your skill level right away. Let's celebrate some success and then push ourselves to the next level. (I find this is also true in everyday life . . .)

- Be consistent. Keep a consistent temperature and clean smoke throughout your cook. That's the goal. That's the skill. That's the work.

- Do it your way. Once you have some smoking under your belt, I encourage you to create your own techniques and incorporate your own ideas. You'll know your equipment and its tendencies better than anyone—plus, it's easier to remember the stuff you make up yourself!

- Avoid injections. Yes, I know on page 25 I tell you we use injections for our competition BBQ. However, the injections create such a strong flavor that it's tough to eat a full plate of food—which is typically how the backyard barbecue works!

- Presentation matters. While your family and neighbors might not be giving you a score, chances are they are more likely to be impressed by your barbecue if it looks good on the plate.

COMPETITION-STYLE ST. LOUIS SPARE RIBS

A backyard party favorite, these ribs are a favorite of barbecue judges as well! At KCBS (Kansas City Barbecue Society) events, we always cook St. Louis–style spare ribs. They are bigger and meatier; they square up easier and lay flatter than baby back ribs. We have been able to win over KCBS judges using this particular recipe—even winning a Kansas State Championship.

Total time: 4 hours 30 minutes

6 slabs St. Louis–style spare ribs

2 cups (384 g) Meat Mitch Competition WHOMP! Rub, store-bought or homemade (see page 28)

2 cups (450 g) packed light brown sugar

1 squeeze bottle (12 ounces, or 355 ml) Parkay Squeeze Vegetable Oil Soft Spread

2 bottles (21 ounces, or 595 g each) or 4 cups (1.1 kg) Meat Mitch Competition WHOMP! BBQ Sauce, store-bought or homemade (see page 32)

Greens (see page 24)

Fire up your smoker to 225°F (107°C) with a good smoke rolling and get ready for battle. We are smoking spare ribs today, kids. Let's get fired up!

First, take a paper towel and pat down your ribs; this will remove any bone fragments that might be on the meat. Flip the slab over and use another paper towel to help you pull the membrane off the bones. Use a small knife and slide it up along the first bone, nudging up the membrane. This should give you the opportunity to grab the membrane with your paper towel. Grab it and pull the membrane across the ribs, removing it all in one swoop. Done. Repeat for all the slabs.

You have to look at your racks and eye them up for problems, such as jagged bones hanging off the edges or big chunks of meat hanging off the side. Take a sharp knife and remove any excess fat on top—you aren't Edward Scissorhands, so less cutting is more and be careful. Flip the rack over and try to square up any extra meat to make the rack cleanly and sharply shaped.

recipe continues

Next, evenly cover with the Meat Mitch Competition WHOMP! Rub on the top, bottom, and sides. Don't overly season. These aren't your huge proteins, and they don't need as much season love.

Now, let rest for 30 minutes at room temperature to allow the slabs to sweat.

It's time to climb aboard the smoker. Hold both ends of each slab and press them together a little bit; then, put them on the grate in the smoker in a single layer, bone-side down and meat-side up. Now's the time to feed the fire with some unlit charcoal and chunks of pecan. Pecan is an amazing flavor for these ribs. Let the ribs cook and soak up the pecan for 3 hours, maintaining the temperature at 225°F (107°C) and maintaining the smoke from the pecan. After 3 hours, look for the bark. You want that deep, mahogany, crusty yumminess.

BARK

Is there anything more delicious than the burnt ends of barbecue brisket? I'm talking about the deep, dark, sweet, salty, melt-in-your-mouth, absolutely-not-burnt morsels of brisket crust made from a combination of the spice rub crust on the meat plus smoke. Whenever we barbecue, we are looking for the bark, the crust on the meat—whether it's beef or pork. One of the reasons ribs are so popular is the high ratio of bark to meat.

Now, it's time to play a little. Place the slabs on separate pieces of foil, sprinkle brown sugar over your ribs, and then have fun squirting that blue bottle of Parkay across the tops. Don't be shy. Close the foil and place the ribs back in the smoker, which should still be at 225°F (107°C).

After another hour, take a peek. You should see the meat starting to retreat up the bones. You should be able to pinch the meat in between the bones to feel for tenderness. (I never check the temperature of the meat, but I might now just be getting old.) Just don't overcook—because anyone can do that. You want them perfect so when you take a bite, your mark is perfectly framed in the rib.

When you have them like you want them, open up the foil, release the steam, and drain off the juice. Now, roll up the sides of the foil and create what I like to call a boat for the ribs. Take your brush and apply a light coating of Meat Mitch Competition WHOMP! BBQ Sauce to both sides of the ribs. Return the ribs in their boats to the smoker for 15 minutes to allow the sauce to set up.

Finish with a quick pass on the grill. Place the ribs meat-side down directly over the fire and grill only for about a minute.

Now, it's time to cut and serve. Set the ribs on the cutting board meat-side down so you can see the bones. Cut each slab into six ribs, cutting between the bones.

To set up a box for judging, determine which are best slabs and grab six consecutive ribs from each slab. Over the greens in the box, layer six ribs across with six more layered on top. Loaded is loyal—fill your box up and let the judges know you ain't scared and let your backyard buddies know who's boss!

Serves 12 to 18 people

COMPETITION-STYLE PULLED PORK

Behold—a beautiful, mahogany pork butt, falling apart and melting into your mouth. Hints of salt, sweet, and peppery bark stare at you, begging to be eaten. Light pink and cherry red hues from the smoke ring always make me smile and always make me hungry. With this cook, you want to make sure you pay attention to the trimming and expose and shape the money muscle to prepare for presentation.

Fire up your smoker to 225°F (107°C) with a good smoke rolling and get ready for battle. Let's get fired up!

The meat will have a big fat cap on it, and you should trim that down to a thin layer. The meat contains a large amount of fat throughout, so don't worry about it drying out; it will be plenty moist.

Then, you need to focus on the money muscle, trimming the meat to look like a log, which exposes as much money muscle as possible for seasoning, smoke, and bark.

Total time: 9 to 10 hours

10- to 12-pound (4.5 to 5.5 kg) bone-in pork butt (Boston butt)

1 cup (192 g) Meat Mitch Competition WHOMP! Rub, store-bought or homemade (see page 28)

1 cup (235 ml) pork injection, mixed according to the package directions (see page 25) (optional, for competition only)

Apple juice

1 bottle (16 ounces, or 340 g) Stubb's Pork Marinade (optional)

1 bottle (21 ounces, or 595 g) Meat Mitch WHOMP! Naked BBQ Sauce

1 tablespoon (20 g) honey

Greens (see page 24)

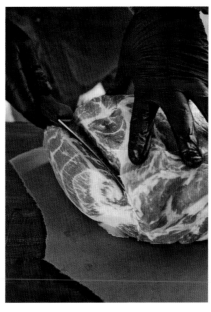

recipe continues

Once you have trimmed the meat, it's time to inject. Pick your favorite from among those I have listed on page 25. This is the fun part—load up your injector or syringe and pump that bad boy full of juice, injecting it randomly all over the meat, until it is packed full.

After you have loaded it up, make sure to pat the meat dry with paper towels. Then, cover liberally in Meat Mitch Competition WHOMP! Rub and let it sit for about 30 minutes to sweat.

With your meat ready and your smoker rolling at 225°F (107°C), place your meat inside the smoker. Feed the fire with some unlit charcoal and chunks of pecan and cherry. Close it up and make sure you have plenty of Royal Oak charcoal and pecan and cherry wood. You'll be smoking for approximately 6 hours.

Every 30 minutes, open up the smoker and spray the meat with apple juice. (Put about ½ cup [120 ml] of apple juice in a spray bottle for this.) After about 6 hours, check the meat to see if you've achieved that mahogany bark.

When this bark is achieved, lay the pork on a big sheet of aluminum foil. Pour the Stubbs Pork Marinade around the base of the meat, close up the foil, and return the meat to the smoker. This step essentially steams the meat and breaks it down to achieve the tenderness you want; keep the smoker at 225°F (107°C). This stage usually lasts 3 hours, but it can always vary depending on the weather, the meat, and the gods. At the end of the cook, you are watching for internal temperature to reach the target goal of 197°F (92°C). You don't want it so tender that the money muscle falls apart. Remove the meat from the pit and open up the foil to let out the steam. Then, close it back up and place it in a dry cooler to rest for at least an hour. (I have let it rest for up to 4 hours, and it was great.)

Next, doctor up your barbecue sauce. Take a bottle of Meat Mitch WHOMP! Naked BBQ Sauce and pour it into a pan along with enough apple juice and honey to thin the sauce and make it slightly sweeter. Also, the honey adds to the shine. Remember, judges eat with their eyes first. Heat the pan on the back of the smoker box, making sure to stir frequently so it does not burn.

Finally, it's time to break down the meat. Carefully carve out the money muscle, keeping it as a perfectly shaped loaf, move it to a separate pan, and cover it with foil to keep it warm.

It's time to remove the bone. It should slide out easily and clean—if so, job well done! Chunk the remaining meat, paying close attention to the bark, trying to capture the best pieces. Separate the meat into nice barky chunks and tubes and then pull and slightly shred the remaining pork. Lightly glaze the meat with sauce, making sure not to add too much. Cover the pan with foil and set aside.

Turn your attention to the money muscle. Brush the muscle with sauce; add just a light coating. It should glisten with the honey in the sauce. Next, carefully slice it into six even pieces (remember, six judges), but make sure to keep the loaf shape intact.

To assemble the judges' box, start with the arranged greens in the box. Then, place the money muscle slices along the back of the box and fill in the front of the box with chunks on one side and pulled pork on the other side. You are ready for turn in! (If you're serving it in your backyard, drop it on the picnic table and watch your neighbors fight it out.)

Serves 12 to 14

COMPETITION-STYLE CHICKEN THIGHS

Competition chicken is a lot harder than you might think. Chicken doesn't take a lot of time to cook, but it does take a lot of time to prepare. The bite-through skin is everything. But have you seen raw chicken skin? There's nothing bite-through about it! To prepare the skin the way we do, you will need a multi-blade handheld meat tenderizer. We like the Jaccard Meat Maximizer Meat Tenderizer, which has 45 blades that plunge all the way through a steak, chop, or piece of chicken. While the blades don't flatten meat like a mallet-style tenderizer, the meat will get a little thinner as it relaxes and spreads out. I love to douse these thighs in a spicy, sweet Candy Sauce. Let's get to work.

Fire up your smoker to 225°F (107°C) with a good smoke rolling.

Chicken thighs are a lot of work, mainly because you have to pay a lot of attention to the skin. Judges are looking for bite-through skin when they taste your product—and you need to give it to them. Start by removing the skins of the thighs. Here is where it becomes tedious. Using an extra sharp, thin knife, carefully scrape the underneath part of the skin—thinning it out and removing excess fat and skin. You want to make the skin as thin as possible without ripping it. *Be careful.*

When finished, use a multi-blade handheld meat tenderizer to put small perforations in the skin. While the skins are off, shape the thighs and then the skin to fit on top of the thigh perfectly.

Next, place the skin back on the thigh. Coat each thigh evenly with the WHOMP! Rub.

Once you have your smoker rolling at 225°F (107°C), open the smoker and add a combination of pecan and apple wood chunks. Gently place the thighs on the grates, keeping a decent amount of space between them. You never want them touching. This is a quick smoke; 45 minutes and you are done.

Then, it's time for a Candy Sauce bath. Doesn't that sound money! Fill a foil pan with the Candy Sauce and place the chicken in the bath, skin-side up. Cover tightly with foil, place on top of the fire, and boil for 20 minutes. (If your smoker isn't fitted with a grate on top of the firebox, you'll have to do it in a separate grill.)

Remove the chicken from the bath and place the thighs, uncovered, on top of a grate that rests on a sheet pan. Allow to rest while the BBQ Sauce is prepared.

While the chicken rests, combine the Meat Mitch Competition WHOMP! BBQ Sauce with the honey in a saucepan and heat gently until the sauce is hot and the honey has melted into the sauce. Thin it down with a little apple juice.

recipe continues

Total time: 90 minutes

16 bone-in chicken thighs (I prefer the Smart Chicken brand)

1½ cups (288 g) Meat Mitch Competition WHOMP! Rub, store-bought or homemade (see page 28)

1¼ gallons (5 L) Candy Sauce (see page 29)

1 bottle (21 ounces, or 595 g) Meat Mitch Competition WHOMP! BBQ Sauce store-bought or homemade (see page 32)

12 ounce (340 g) jar of honey honey

1 to 2 tablespoons (15 to 28 ml) apple juice

Next, you'll quickly grill on a raised grate over fire; ideally, the grate is 2 inches (5 cm) above a low fire, and don't forget to oil the grate so the skin doesn't stick to it. Here what you want to do is set and crisp the skin. Grill it briefly on both sides but watch carefully; you don't want to burn it or shrivel the skin. Once you feel you have achieved a crisp finish to the skin, brush on a light layer of the heated Meat Mitch Competition WHOMP! BBQ Sauce. Put six of the best thighs in the box with the greens. This will be a fan favorite with friends and family. It's not every day folks get to sink their teeth into chicken thighs packed with this much flavor and manicured for the Hollywood runway!

Makes 16 chicken thighs

COMPETITION-STYLE BEEF BRISKET AND BURNT ENDS

When I enter a competition for brisket, I want a 16-pound (7.3 kg) Wagyu brisket. It's time to pay the piper. These bad boys aren't cheap. Generally, they run around $165 a piece, but are well worth it, if you want to win. If you aren't willing to spend that kind of dough, the next best thing is to age your brisket. You can keep it in the vacuum packaging in a seldom-opened refrigerator in your basement. If you can find the kill date (see packaging or ask the butcher), you can go 40 days past that date, and you'll be able to trim it with a butter knife.

Fire up your smoker to 225°F (107°C) and get a good smoke rolling.

As with everything, trimming is key. There will be a layer of fat on the brisket. Trim this down to ¼ inch (6 mm). Flip over and remove any excess fat and silverskin with a sharp knife. You want to shape the brisket now so that when it has finished cooking, it will be the desired size you want for the judge's box. This avoids having to make extra cuts on your brisket slices later just to fit inside the box. It's important to look at the direction of the grain. Usually, this will run diagonally to a corner point. Take your knife and make a slice directly across the grain, marking it. After the cook, it isn't as easy to see the grain, so making this cut lets you know exactly how to slice. Trim and separate the point from the flat. The point is the portion you'll use to make your burnt ends.

Next, if you are in a competition, it is time to inject. Plan to do so in a 1-inch (2.5 cm) grid formation as you cover the entire flat and point. Once completed, wipe down the meat and dry with paper towels.

It's time to rub that baby down with Meat Mitch Steer Season Rub. This rub was designed for brisket, and it wears it like a fur coat. These big proteins can take the rub, so don't be shy, just be consistent in your coating.

Now, it's time for the smoker at 225°F (107°C) with a good smoke rolling. Enter the brisket (Cue Metallica's "Enter Sandman") and add additional charcoal and pecan and cherry wood. Plan to smoke for approximately 6 hours with pecan and cherry wood. (I don't use the post oak that's famous in Texas; I use what I like the best.)

After about 6 hours, you are looking for one thing: that bark. How does it look? We want that deep mahogany, salty crust.

Once you have achieved that, set both the point and the flat on a piece of aluminum foil and tackle the tenderness. Add the Campbell's Condensed Beef Consommé around the base in the foil, wrap it up, and return it to the smoker to steam for about 3 hours.

recipe continues

Total time: 9 to 10 hours

16-pound (7.3 kg) whole packer Wagyu beef brisket (see Tip on page 58)

1 cup (192 g) Meat Mitch Steer Season Rub, store-bought or homemade (see page 31)

1 cup (235 ml) beef injection made per package instructions (see page 25) (optional; for competition only)

1 can (10.5 ounces, or 300 ml) Campbell's Condensed Beef Consommé

1 cup (192 g) Meat Mitch Competition WHOMP! BBQ Sauce, store-bought or homemade (see page 30)

½ cup (118 ml) apple juice

2 tablespoons (42 g) honey

Check in about 3 hours for an internal temperature of 205°F (96°C). When it hits that, remove it from the smoker, open up the foil, and release the steam. Wrap 'em back up and place in an insulated food bag to rest for at least an hour and up to 4 hours.

While the brisket rests, combine the Meat Mitch Competition WHOMP! BBQ Sauce with the honey in a saucepan and heat gently until the sauce is hot and the honey has melted into the sauce. Thin it down with a little apple juice.

It's time to prep for turn in. Brush a thin coating of the thinned barbecue sauce on both the point and the flat. Then take the flat, find the marked end, and make slices across the grain in a line with the mark that you made. You want the cuts to be the thickness of a pencil eraser.

Then, lay the slices out and paint one side (the side the judges won't see) of each slice with a light coating of sauce. Take at least six slices and place them on the greens in the box, layering them on top of each other (like a bacon package), showing the smoke ring that you worked so hard for on each slice.

Next, tackle the burnt ends. Cut 1-inch (2.5 cm) square cubes from the remaining meat, and of course, sample them. If it melts like cotton candy, the way it is supposed to, put some in the box. (I like to line them up side by side in a straight line in the front of the box—at least six pieces). If the piece doesn't melt in your mouth, then don't put the burnt ends in the box—that's the rule. Your brisket box is complete! And, if these make it from your smoker to the backyard, your friends are lucky. These are the prize of Kansas City.

TIP: Buy a whole packer brisket, which includes both the flat and the point of the brisket connected and in one piece. Use the flat for the brisket slices and the point to make your burnt ends.

Serves 10 to 12

JERRY'S BROWN SUGAR SMOKED PORK SAUSAGE

This sausage from teammate Jerry Knearem is a fan favorite at our American Royal World Series of Barbecue parties. People rave over our sausage. If you are going to make sausage, you might as well make a bunch of it! This is a super simple recipe but has won us many awards. (Smoked sausage is a judged category but it doesn't count towards your actual overall competition score.) You'll need to use the grinder attachment and the sausage stuffer kit for your KitchenAid mixer or buy a meat grinder and a sausage stuffer either online or at your closest outdoor store, like Cabela's or Bass Pro Shop. The casings are easily found online as well, just make sure you rinse them out well!

Total time: 2 hours

- 10 pounds (4.6 kg) boneless pork butt, diced
- ½ cup (96 g) A. C. Legg's Old Plantation Spice Blend #10 (see Tip below)
- ¼ cup (60 G) packed light brown sugar, plus more to roll the sausages in
- 2 cups (475 ml) ice water
- 2 or 3 hog casings, totaling 20 to 25 feet (610 to 762 cm)

Toss the meat and A. C. Legg's Old Plantation Spice Blend #10 in a bowl until well mixed. Spread out on sheet pans, cover with plastic wrap, and place in the freezer for about 30 minutes. Grind the mixture through the small (⅛ inch [3 mm]) die. Put the ground meat back in the large mixing bowl, put latex gloves on, and mix the ground meat, brown sugar, and ice water by hand for 1 minute. It will be *cold*, but well worth the pain. The meat should look sticky and smell amazing.

Cover the sausage mix with plastic wrap and place in the refrigerator for 1 hour to chill. Set up your sausage stuffer. While the meat chills, soak your casings to get rid of the salt that preserves them, making sure to change the water a few times.

Fill your sausage stuffer and press down until just a little meat squeezes out of the tip. Slide the entire casing onto the nozzle. Now here's the fun part: start cranking! This takes a little rhythm, but you'll get the hang of it. When you have stuffed it all, pinch the links about 6 inches (15 cm) apart and twist to make the sausages. (This is the size that fits in our judge's boxes.)

Roll the sausages in brown sugar, making sure to coat all over. Smoke at 225 to 250°F (107 to 120°C) until the sausages reach 150°F (66°C) internally, about 45 minutes to 1 hour. Eat right away or cool down completely and then warm them up and char them on a grill when you are ready to serve. Store extra sausages in the refrigerator for up to a week.

TIP: Go to aclegg.com to find a distributor for their Old Plantation Seasoning Blends and Marinades in your area. It's the secret ingredient!

Makes about 40 sausages

Jerry Knearem and Mitch Benjamin at the American Royal World Series of Barbecue.

PAUL PATTERSON

ROSIE'S SMOKEHOUSE
PARIS, FRANCE

I may someday write an entire book about how great Paul Patterson is, but for starters, let's consider my first morning in Paris. I got to Rosie's Smokehouse at 10:30 am, a little early for my first day on a job that was set to begin at 11 am. I was nervous, in a foreign country, and unsure of what I had gotten myself into for the next few months.

Shortly after I arrived at the restaurant, in walked Paul Patterson, the head chef, who—fortunately for me—was from New Zealand and so spoke English. He was tall, thin, with long black curly hair, and wearing a unique black leather Akubra (an Outback-style hat), black leather jacket, and leather boots. Tattoos covered everywhere I could see. Needless to say, we looked nothing alike. He paused when he walked past me and said, "You Mike?" I answered, "I'm Mitch." He said, "Close enough. Follow me."

He spent the morning and afternoon showing me the ropes of the kitchen and smoker and how he prepped to execute the day. I tried to absorb everything as best as I could and mostly listened. Paul was an established chef in Paris with great understanding of multiple cuisines. American barbecue, however, was new to him, and that's why I was there.

At 3 pm the first day, he dropped his ponytail, put back on his leather jacket and hat, and changed from sneakers back into his leather boots. "What's going on?" I asked. He said, "It's 3 pm, mate. We are now closed." I asked, "What do we do now?" He said, "We go on a walkabout, so grab your shit!" We proceeded to walk up and down the streets of St. Michel and jump from bar to bar, where Paul knew everyone. Beers and shots were on the house, and people seemed very happy to meet me. (This was amazing!) Just shy of 6 pm, Paul announced that we were heading back to the restaurant. We needed to open up! That was my new French-style 8-hour workday—11 am to 3 pm, close, go on walkabout with Paul from 3 pm to 6 pm, and then reopen from 6 pm to 10 pm. Wash down the kitchen and work space and then out the door for the night back to Paul's friends and pubs. That night I said to Paul, "This is too much fun. How often will it be like this?" He replied, "Every day, mate!" This was a whole new world for me, and Paul was there for the next few months to

Photo by Mili Villamil Photography, courtesy of Paul Patterson

guide me through it every step of the way. Of course, I was also able to quickly teach Paul and the Rosie's team how to approach, prep, and execute great Kansas City barbecue.

In an effort to return Paul's unparalleled generosity and friendship, we hatched a plan to bring him back with me to the United States in May. We would spend a week in Kansas City with my family and then a week in Tennessee competing with my team at the Memphis in May World Championship Barbecue Cooking Contest. It was truly a storybook ending because our team earned a trip to the grand stage by winning two trophies, including one in the seafood category, which Paul was in charge of!

SMOKED BUTTER & WHISKEY SEAFOOD ROLL

RECIPE BY PAUL PATTERSON, MEMPHIS IN MAY WINNER

When it came to the Memphis in May World Championship Barbecue Cooking Contest in Tennessee, Paul and I had been planning this adventure for the previous month. Paul knew he was in charge of our entry for the seafood category. After much experimenting and tons of whiskey, this little beauty won Paul and our team a trip up onto center stage to receive the big winning trophy! When you start with smoked butter and add garlic, shrimp, crabmeat, and whiskey . . . C'mon, mate!

1 cup (225 g, or 2 sticks) unsalted butter

½ red onion, diced

3 cloves garlic, crushed

¼ cup (60 ml) Jack Daniel's (or whatever whiskey you have open)

3 jalapeños, stemmed, seeded, and sliced

1 pound (455 g) lump crab meat, drained

1 quart (946 ml) heavy cream

12 (16/20-size) shrimp, each cut into four pieces

1 lime, halved

2 tablespoons (35 g) Meat Mitch Competition WHOMP! BBQ Sauce, store-bought or homemade (see page 32)

1 package white hotdog buns (nothing fancy)

To smoke the butter, set your smoker to 225°F (107°C) and get a good smoke rolling. Put the butter in a small cast iron pot and place it inside the smoker to allow the smoke to roll over the melting butter and permeate it. Allow as much time as you can for the butter to melt, not burn, and to absorb the smoky air. For the competition, we smoked it for 45 minutes.

Over a gas or charcoal grill or burner on your stove, heat a pan over medium heat. Add the smoked butter, red onion, garlic, and jalapeños and sweat for about 10 minutes or until soft. Pull the pan off of the heat and add the Jack Daniel's. Return to the stove and burn off the alcohol for about 1 minute over medium-high heat. Be careful, Podsy! Jack Daniels burns in the pan as sweet as it does going down the hatch.

Add the crabmeat, cream, and squeeze half of the lime into mix. Now for the best part—pour in Meat Mitch Competition WHOMP! BBQ Sauce and then simmer until thick, 3 or 4 minutes. Once it's thick, add the shrimp and then cook down for another 5 minutes or so until thick like chili.

Brush the hotdog buns (the secret to winning in Memphis is to keep it simple, never go fancy!) with the rest of the smoked butter and fill. Don't even think about waiting to eat these. Winners win!

Serves 8

SMOKED BACON AND BRISKET PIE

RECIPE BY PAUL PATTERSON

Pies in New Zealand range from a small hand pie to regular-sized pies, and they fill them with anything and everything! They are also available everywhere, including in all the roadside convenience stores, so you can grab and go. This recipe is inspired by the best of those pies, which we ate through my entire trip.

Crank your oven up to 350°F (180°C, or gas mark 4) with a rack in the middle of the oven. If you have a convection fan, it's great to turn it on for this pie.

In a medium pot, cook the bacon over medium-low heat until crisp, about 10 minutes. Drain off most of the fat and save for something delicious later. Toss in the onion and garlic with the olive oil and sauté over low heat until translucent, 5 to 8 minutes.

Add the beef stock, Worcestershire sauce, Meat Mitch Competition WHOMP! BBQ Sauce, and smoked paprika and simmer for 8 to 10 minutes until reduced a little bit.

Gently stir in the smoked brisket and simmer for an additional 5 to 8 minutes until slightly thick.

Season to taste with salt and pepper. Depending on the thickness of the meat filling, you may wish to add 1 tablespoon (8 g) of cornstarch to the stock base to help thicken your filling. Set your filling aside to cool for 10 to 15 minutes while you prepare your pastry.

Line the bottom of a quarter-sheet pan with one sheet of puff pastry, using more if needed to patch any tears in the dough. Fill with the brisket mix and then top with the cheeses. Make a "lid" with more of the puff pastry, making sure that it drapes over the edges, and press to seal. Brush the pie lid with the egg wash. Using a sharp, 4-inch (10 cm) paring knife, slice a 1-inch (2.5 cm) X shape exactly in the middle of the lid of the pie to allow steam to escape.

Bake until golden brown and hot, rotating once, about 15 minutes. Let cool to around room temperature and serve.

Serves 6

⅓ pound (150 g) smoked bacon, diced

1 onion, minced

3 cloves garlic, crushed

1 tablespoon (15 ml) extra-virgin olive oil

1½ cups (355 ml) beef stock

2 tablespoons (35 g) Meat Mitch Competition WHOMP! BBQ Sauce, store-bought or homemade (see page 32)

1 tablespoon (15 ml) Worcestershire sauce

¼ teaspoon smoked paprika

⅔ pound (300 g) smoked beef brisket (see Competition-Style Beef Brisket and Burnt Ends, page 57), shredded or diced

Freshly ground black pepper

Kosher salt

1 tablespoon (8 g) cornstarch (optional)

3 to 4 sheets puff pastry, thawed if frozen

½ cup (58 g) shredded smoked cheddar

½ cup (60 g) shredded Gouda

1 egg, beaten for egg wash

2

CHAR BAR SMOKED MEATS & AMUSEMENTS

When you walk into Char Bar Smoked Meats & Amusements, a pleasant aroma of burning hickory immediately hits your nose. Looking up, you'll spy the chefs in the open kitchen. Walking past the front of an old Buick, you make your way out to the backyard beer garden. You grab a seat at the fire pit and settle in for a predinner drink: a snifter of our famous cocktail, The Smoking Gun . . . wait a minute! Where was I? Oh yeah, when I last left you with my story on page 16, I was but a humble weekend BBQ warrior. And now, here I am with a restaurant! I guess I should tell you how that happened and what Char Bar Smoked Meats & Amusements is all about.

After years on the competition circuit and with experience creating a line of sauces and rubs under my belt, there was no denying the direction my life was headed. It was only natural to start daydreaming about a restaurant. But how would I get from point A to point B? I didn't know jack about restaurants except that most of them go out of business in the first two years. Luckily, one of my teammates, Cory Lagerstrom, believed in me. He introduced me to James Westphal and Mark Kelpe, two successful restauranteurs in Kansas City. After we met, it was clear: they knew restaurants and I knew BBQ. It was a match made in heaven!

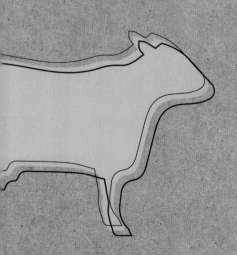

It took a year-and-a-half of work before we were ready to open though. We spent that time hunting for the perfect location, arguing about the name, figuring out logos and design, taking architect and contractor meetings, and of course, testing dishes for the menu. There were ups and downs along the way. In the eleventh hour, we lost our location and had to pivot. We got lucky and ended up inheriting a dream location—an iconic space that used to be a country western music venue known as the Beaumont Club. (I can still remember seeing Blake Shelton play there before he was a mega-superstar . . . he still had a mullet!) What the Beaumont Club gave us was built-in character and an endless amount of space to play with, both inside and out.

My two partners, along with Dan Salazar, an interior design artist, pored over every detail. The theme we ran with was "burnt, charred, seared, scorched, or smoked" with retro carnival objects and vintage amusements. Our goal was to keep things *fun*. They designed a dining room that sits down at a lower level with handmade leather booths and several welcoming tables—assembled using charred ash and razed bowling alley lanes that Mark found in a warehouse in Brooklyn. There is an enormous mural on the south wall that portrays an old-school backyard cookout. Lights the shape of gas pumps hang down over dining tables, with bulbs flickering like fire. We managed to keep some of the original exposed brick and the ceiling is painted black, with an amazing array of small lights carefully positioned to portray the look of burning embers.

The Char Bar team: Jeremy Tawney, Mark Kelpe, Mitch Benjamin, James Westphal, and Michael Peterson.

Large sliding glass doors completely open up the restaurant to the outside and an enormous fire pit. To me, the exterior was an opportunity to deliver on some of the "amusements." A huge patio, picnic tables, lawn croquet, ping pong tables, bocce ball court on crushed white oyster shells, corn hole, fire pits—and of course an amazing bar and great music. That was the dream and now we have it all. (In fact, I think we now have the largest outdoor barbecue playground in the Midwest!)

By November of 2014, Char Bar Smoked Meats & Amusements was ready to greet the world. I admit, I was nervous as hell. It felt like I was inviting the entire city to pass judgment on my food. Luckily, it all worked out and the year we opened, we even ended up being named the Best New Restaurant in Kansas City by *The Pitch* magazine in their "Best of KC" issue! In this chapter, I'll be joined by Mark Kelpe, and we'll take you on a tour of the dishes that put us on the map. We'll heap up the meats and share the recipe for our incredible Burnt Heaven sandwich. You'll learn how to make the perfect Charred Bits & Grits for your next brunch. Think it's crazy to smoke chicken before making chicken nuggets? Think again! We've included all the sides that people can't seem to get enough of, including Cheesy "Hushpuppies" and the unique Roots & Fruits salad. And we'll even show you how to smoke cocktails like we do at the restaurant! Have fun with us as we introduce you to our team, our personality, and our one-of-a-kind cuisine.

The Char Bar interior.

THE SMOKING GUN

We wanted to offer at least one "smoked" cocktail on Char Bar's beverage menu, so my partner Mark Kelpe created this show-stopper utilizing rye, Grand Marnier, Campari, and a handheld cocktail smoker. Usually, as soon as one Smoking Gun cocktail gets carried through the dining room, there are several more quickly ordered by thirsty patrons. We recommend using the Smoking Gun Pro Handheld Cocktail Smoker, which is available online, for the smoke. And, of course, you can replace the Bulleit rye in the recipe with your favorite rye, but I believe that every "gun" needs a "Bulleit."

2 ounces (60 ml) Bulleit rye

½ ounce (15 ml) Grand Marnier

½ ounce (15 ml) Campari

½ ounce (15 ml) brown sugar syrup (recipe follows)

3 dashes angostura bitters

2 dashes orange bitters

1 large ice sphere

1 orange peel, for garnish

Combine the rye, Grand Marnier, Campari, and brown sugar syrup in a pint glass or cocktail shaker. Add the angostura bitters and orange bitters. Add 3 regular ice cubes and stir with a long bar spoon until cold, about 30 seconds.

Place the frozen ice sphere into a large 16-ounce (475 ml) brandy glass. Pour the strained cocktail into the glass. Place the orange peel on top of the ice sphere.

Using a handheld cocktail smoker according to its manufacturer's directions, emit smoke into brandy glass until completely filled. Quickly place a bar coaster on top of the glass to contain the smoke. Let sit for 30 seconds and serve.

Makes 1 smoky cocktail that might even cause Jesse James to turn and run

BROWN SUGAR SYRUP

1½ cups (355 ml) water

1 pound (455 g, or 2 packed cups) dark brown sugar

Bring the water and sugar to a boil in a saucepan over medium-high heat. Stir constantly for 3 minutes and then reduce the heat to low. Keep stirring until all the sugar dissolves. Remove from the heat and let cool at room temperature. Store excess simple syrup in the refrigerator for up to 1 month.

Makes 2 cups (475 ml)

SMOKED CHICKEN NUGGETS

Chicken nuggets! Who doesn't like chicken nuggets?! But as everyone knows, it's sometimes just as much about the array of dipping sauces as it is about the nuggets themselves. I love my condiments. So, we set out to create a starter of lightly smoked, buttermilk-breaded chicken nuggets with four delicious dipping sauces that even the pickiest of children (and adults) cannot refuse.

Set your smoker to 170°F (77°C) and get a good smoke rolling. Spray the provided wire cooling rack with nonstick cooking spray.

Pat the chicken tenders dry with a paper towel and gently tap to slightly flatten the meat. Season with the 1 teaspoon of salt and black pepper. Smoke for 20 minutes until the outside of the chicken looks opaque, but the interior is still raw. Refrigerate the chicken until completely chilled.

Set up a breading station using three pie pans or shallow bowls. Fill one pan with 2 cups (250 g) of the flour. Fill a second pan with buttermilk and beaten eggs; whisk to combine. Fill a third shallow pan with the remaining 5 cups (625 g) of all-purpose flour mixed with the Meat Mitch All-Purpose Rub. Line a baking sheet with parchment paper.

Cut each jumbo chicken tender into quarters. Dredge each chicken nugget in the plain flour, then in the buttermilk-egg wash, and finally in the seasoned flour. Place on the baking sheet. Loosely cover and refrigerate for at least 1 hour or overnight.

Heat 2 inches (5 cm) of vegetable oil in a large saucepan over medium heat until a deep-fry thermometer registers 350°F (180°C). Place a sheet pan lined with a wire rack in the oven and preheat to 170°F (77°C).

Working in batches, fry the chicken nuggets, turning, until golden brown on all sides and the internal temperature reaches 165°F (74°C), 8 to 10 minutes. Remove with a slotted spoon and drain on paper towels; season with kosher salt.

Keep the fried nuggets warm in the oven on the prepared sheet pan until all frying is complete. Serve with the assortment of four dipping sauces.

Makes about 32 nuggets, or enough to feed your whole flock

16 ounces (455 g) chicken tenders (roughly 8 jumbo tenders)

1 teaspoon kosher salt, plus more for finish

½ teaspoon freshly ground black pepper

7 cups (875 g) all-purpose flour

2 cups (475 ml) buttermilk

2 eggs, beaten

½ cup (96 g) Meat Mitch All-Purpose Rub (see page 28)

1 quart (946 ml) vegetable oil, for frying

¾ cup (168 g) 'Bama White Sauce (recipe follows)

¾ cup (180 g) Barbecue Ranch (recipe follows)

¾ cup (204 g) Carolina Gold Sauce (recipe follows)

¾ cup (198 g) Char Bar Table Sauce, store-bought or homemade (see page 29)

'BAMA WHITE SAUCE

1½ cups (340 g) mayonnaise (I prefer Duke's)

¼ cup (60 ml) apple cider vinegar

2 tablespoons (30 g) prepared horseradish

1 tablespoon (15 g) spicy brown mustard

1 tablespoon (13 g) sugar

½ teaspoon kosher salt

½ teaspoon freshly ground black pepper

¼ teaspoon garlic powder

¼ teaspoon ground cayenne

Alabama white sauce was made famous by Big Bob Gibson in Decatur, Alabama. Chris Lilly is their pitmaster, and he is one of the most accomplished and celebrated barbecue chefs in the world. He's also my buddy, and I was fortunate enough to host Chris and his team at Char Bar following an The American Royal World Series of Barbecue event. He approved of my 'Bama White Sauce! It's creamy, rich, and tangy with just a slight kiss of heat from the cayenne pepper. This sauce is delicious drizzled over smoked bone-in chicken and makes a great dipping sauce for our crispy Smoked Chicken Nuggets.

In a small bowl, stir together all the ingredients until well combined. Use immediately or refrigerate for up to 2 weeks.

Makes 2 cups (448 g)

CAROLINA GOLD

¾ cup (132 g) yellow mustard

½ cup (120 ml) apple cider vinegar

½ cup (170 g) honey

2 packed (30 g) tablespoons light brown sugar

2 tablespoons (30 g) ketchup

1 teaspoon Worcestershire sauce

1 teaspoon garlic powder

½ teaspoon kosher salt

¼ teaspoon freshly ground black pepper

Our pitmaster, Jeremy Tawney, created this a riff on South Carolina's famous vinegar-based yellow barbecue sauce. It's a little sweet from the honey and a little tangy from the apple cider vinegar. It's great glazed over grilled chicken thighs or tossed with pulled pork and served on bread with coleslaw. It also makes a great dipping sauce for our crispy Smoked Chicken Nuggets. Heck, I can eat an entire bag of pretzels dipped in it!

Combine all the ingredients in a small saucepan and stir until well combined. Cook over low heat, stirring continuously for 5 to 7 minutes, until the mixture reaches a low simmer.

Cool completely. Serve immediately or transfer to a jar and refrigerate for up to 2 weeks.

Makes 2 cups (544 g)

BARBECUE RANCH

1 cup (225 g) mayonnaise
(I prefer Duke's)

½ cup (230 g) sour cream

½ cup (132 g) Char Bar Table
Sauce, store-bought or
homemade (see page 29)

1 packet (3 tablespoons)
Hidden Valley Original Ranch
Seasoning Mix

1 packed tablespoon (15 g) light
brown sugar

1 tablespoon (15 ml) Tabasco
sauce

At Char Bar, this tangy sauce is smeared on our famous Burnt Heaven and our charred Salmon BLT Club and is used as one of the four colorful dipping sauces for our crispy Smoked Chicken Nuggets. What doesn't taste good mixed with ranch seasoning?!

Combine all the ingredients together in a mixing bowl until well combined. Use immediately or refrigerate for up to 2 weeks.

Makes 2 cups (480 g)

THE BURNT HEAVEN

This winning sandwich was created by our pitmaster, Jeremy Tawney. It's something he would make for himself during his days smoking meat as head pitmaster at the world-famous Oklahoma Joe's. The sandwich is crispy, creamy, smoky, and spicy with every bite. And it's been Char Bar's top-selling sandwich since Day One. You gotta have a showstopper! This one is it!

4 potato buns (I prefer Martin's), sliced open

¼ cup (55 g, or ½ stick) unsalted butter, melted

¼ cup (60 g) Barbecue Ranch (see page 77)

8 ounces (225 g) Jerry's Brown Sugar Smoked Pork Sausage (see page 62), warmed

16 ounces (455 g) burnt ends (see Competition-Style Beef Brisket and Burnt Ends, page 57)

1 cup (120 g) Spicy Coleslaw (see page 95)

24 Crispy Jalapeño Strips (recipe follows)

Brush the buns with the melted butter and place buttered-side down on a hot griddle to toast for 2 minutes until golden brown. Spread each bottom bun with 1 tablespoon (15 g) of the Barbecue Ranch.

Slice the warm sausage ½-inch (1.3 cm) thick and evenly arrange 4 to 5 slices on each bottom bun to form a foundation. Carefully pile the warm burnt ends as high as possible on the sausage. Top each sandwich with ¼ cup (30 g) of coleslaw and 6 crispy jalapeño strips and lightly smoosh with the top bun.

Serves 4 (Make sure you provide everyone with a bib.)

CRISPY JALAPEÑO STRIPS

2 large jalapeños

2 cups (250 g) all-purpose flour

1 cup (235 ml) buttermilk

2 tablespoons (24 g) Meat Mitch All-Purpose Rub (see page 28)

1 quart (946 ml) vegetable oil, for frying

½ teaspoon kosher salt

Slice each jalapeño in half vertically, remove the stem and seeds, and thinly slice lengthwise into ⅛ inch (3 mm)-thick slices.

Set up a breading station using three pie pans or shallow bowls. Fill one pan with 1 cup (125 g) of the all-purpose flour. Fill the second pan with buttermilk. Fill third shallow pan with the remaining 1 cup (125 g) of all-purpose flour mixed with the Meat Mitch All-Purpose Rub.

Toss the jalapeño strips into the unseasoned all-purpose flour, then dredge through buttermilk, and finally toss in seasoned flour.

Heat 2 inches (5 cm) of vegetable oil in a large saucepan over medium heat until a deep-fry thermometer registers 350°F (180°C). Working in batches, fry the jalapeño strips until golden brown and crispy, 4 to 5 minutes. Remove with a slotted spoon and drain on paper towels; season with kosher salt. Keep warm until serving.

Makes about 24 crispy strips

CHARRED BITS & GRITS

This Char Bar appetizer has become a great way to showcase our famous burnt ends and hand-cranked sausage. The combination of the creamy cheddar grits, sweet candied bacon, and spicy pickled jalapeño is a match made in heaven. This recipe makes four individual servings, but for a barbecue buffet, arrange it all on a single giant party platter and wait for major "ooohs" and "aaahs."

Spoon the grits down the center of each plate. Arrange pieces of burnt ends and smoked sausage slices on top of the grits. Drizzle the BBQ Butter over the grits and pool around edge of plate.

Break each slice of Pig Candy into thirds and arrange vertically stuck in the grits. Garnish with 4 pickled jalapeño slices and 2 pickled shallot slices on each plate. Sprinkle the Pecorino-Romano cheese over the top.

Serves 4 generously or can be combined into one big, beautiful, bodacious buffet platter

4 cups (1 kg) White Cheddar Grits (see page 82), warm

12 ounces (340 g) burnt ends (see Competition-Style Beef Brisket and Burnt Ends, page 57)

8 ounces (225 g) Jerry's Brown Sugar Smoked Pork Sausage (see page 62), sliced ¼-inch (6mm) thick

1¼ cups (295 ml) BBQ Butter (recipe follows)

4 slices Pig Candy (see page 165)

16 pickled jalapeño slices (recipe follows)

8 slices pickled shallot (recipe follows)

1 ounce (28 g) Pecorino-Romano cheese, grated

BBQ BUTTER

1 cup (264 g) Char Bar Table Sauce, store-bought or homemade (see page 32)

½ cup (112 g, or 1 stick) unsalted butter, cut into pats

In a small saucepan, heat the sauce over medium heat to a simmer. Remove from the heat and gently whisk in the butter pats, one at a time, until combined. Serve warm.

Makes 1¼ cups (295 ml)

PICKLED JALAPEÑOS AND SHALLOTS

1 cup (235 ml) water

1 cup (235 ml) rice wine vinegar

2 tablespoons (26 g) sugar

2 whole jalapeños, stemmed, seeded, and sliced ¼-inch (6 mm) thick

1 shallot, julienned

These also make a great topping for burgers.

Combine the water, rice wine vinegar, and sugar in small saucepan over medium heat, bring to rapid boil, and then turn off heat. Chill until ice cold. Add the sliced jalapeño and shallot to the cold pickling liquid and refrigerate overnight.

Makes about ½ cup (150 g) pickled veggies

WHITE CHEDDAR GRITS

Grits may be foreign to some, but they are an absolute fixture on the Southern table. We consider the Anson Mills' stone-ground heirloom grits from South Carolina to be the very best. My grandmother grew up in Gaffney, South Carolina, and she would serve me cheese grits every time I stayed with her. She called them Jimmy Carter grits, and I loved them! Whether serving cheddar grits for breakfast, as a barbecue side, or whipping them up for our Cheesy "Hushpuppies" (see page 83), you'll develop a fondness for them in no time.

6 ounces (170 g, or 1 cup) coarse white grits (I prefer Anson Mills)

4½ cups (1.1 L) cold water

½ teaspoon kosher salt, plus more if needed

3 tablespoons (42 g) unsalted butter

4 ounces (115 g) aged white cheddar (I prefer Tillamook), grated

¼ cup (60 g) sour cream

½ teaspoon freshly ground black pepper

In a medium-size heavy saucepan, combine the grits with 2½ cups (570 ml) of the cold water. Cover the pan and let the grits soak overnight at room temperature.

The next day, set the saucepan over medium heat and bring the mixture to a simmer, stirring constantly with a wooden spoon for 6 minutes. Add the salt, reduce the heat to the lowest possible setting, and cover the pan.

Meanwhile, heat the remaining 2 cups (475 ml) of water in a small saucepan and keep hot. Every 10 minutes or so, uncover the grits and stir them. Each time you find them thick enough to hold the spoon upright, stir in a small amount of the hot water, adding 1½ cups (355 ml) water or more in four or five additions. Cook until the grits are creamy and tender throughout, but not mushy, about 45 minutes.

To finish, remove the grits from the heat and add the butter, cheddar, and sour cream, stirring in with vigorous strokes. Add more salt, if desired, and black pepper.

Serve warm for breakfast or refrigerate overnight and scoop for Cheesy "Hushpuppies" (see page 83).

TIP: Soaking the grits in water overnight reduces their cooking time by almost 50 percent and allows the kernels to better hold their shape. You can skip this step, but will need to double the stovetop cooking time.

Makes about 4 cups (1 kg)

CHEESY "HUSHPUPPIES"

At the time we were developing Char Bar, a crispy appetizer called arancini (fried breaded Italian risotto balls filled with cheese) was all the rage. We thought it would be fun to give this European dish a Southern twist by substituting stone-ground grits for the risotto. We serve these cheesy bites in a pool of "beurre blanc" (a French white wine butter sauce); but sticking to our Southern roots, we substituted a can of PBR lager for the French white wine and call it a "beer blanc." (I'll admit we're suckers for the cheesy pun!) Finally, we top those hushpuppies with an emerald-colored homemade jalapeño jam—it's like waking up in the Land of Oz!

Using a 1-ounce (28 ml) scoop, shape the chilled grits into thirty-two 1-inch (2.5 cm) balls. Line a baking sheet with parchment paper. Set up a breading station using three pie pans or shallow bowls. Fill one pan with the all-purpose flour. Fill the second pan with buttermilk and beaten eggs; whisk to combine. Fill the third shallow pan with the panko breadcrumbs.

Roll each ball in the flour, then in the buttermilk mixture, and finally in the panko breadcrumbs; place on the prepared baking sheet. Loosely cover and refrigerate for at least 1 hour or overnight. (If refrigerating overnight, roll in more panko breadcrumbs before frying).

Heat ½ inch (1 cm) of vegetable oil in a large saucepan over medium heat until a deep-fry thermometer registers 350°F (180°C). Working in batches, fry the hushpuppies, turning, until golden brown on all sides, about 4 minutes. Remove with a slotted spoon and drain on paper towels; season with kosher salt.

To serve, spoon a few tablespoons (45 to 60 ml) of the sauce on each plate and top with the hushpuppies. Top each hushpuppy with the Homemade Jalapeño Jam. Serve immediately.

Makes 32 of the best, crispiest, cheesiest hushpuppies you've ever had

4 cups (1 kg) White Cheddar Grits (see page 82), chilled

2 cups (250 g) all-purpose flour

2 cups (475 ml) buttermilk

2 eggs, beaten

5 cups (560 g) panko breadcrumbs, plus more if needed

1 quart (946 ml) vegetable, oil for frying

Kosher salt

¾ cup (60 ml) Beer Blanc Sauce (recipe follows)

¼ cup (76 g) Homemade Jalapeño Jam (see page 87)

BEER BLANC SAUCE

1 cup (235 ml) Pabst Blue Ribbon beer

¼ cup (60 ml) apple cider vinegar

1 shallot, finely minced

2 cups (475 ml) heavy cream

1 cup (225 g, or 2 sticks) unsalted butter at room temperature, cut into pats

½ teaspoon kosher salt

¼ teaspoon white pepper

In a medium saucepan, combine the beer, vinegar, and shallots over medium heat and simmer until the liquid is reduced down to 2 tablespoons (28 ml).

Add the heavy cream and continue to reduce until you have about ½ cup (120 ml) of sauce remaining. Reduce the heat to very low and whisk in pats of butter, one at a time, whisking slowly until the butter is barely melted. Season with the salt and white pepper. Serve immediately.

Makes 1½ cups (355 ml)

JALAPEÑO-CHEDDAR CORNBREAD MUFFINS

Cornbread isn't boring, trust me . . . well, maybe sometimes it is. But not these muffins! Yes, these little buggers will go fast whether served at a backyard barbecue or your next Sunday family gathering. The jalapeño and Tillamook cheddar cheese set them apart from the norm. Serve them piping hot, slathered with butter and Homemade Jalapeño Jam.

Preheat the oven to 400°F (200°C, or gas mark 6). Grease the cups of a muffin tin.

Combine the cornmeal, flour, sugar, salt, and baking soda in a large bowl and whisk to break up any clumps.

Combine the egg, buttermilk, and melted butter in a medium bowl and whisk to combine.

Add the wet ingredients to dry ingredients and stir until just barely combined. Don't overmix. Gently fold in the jalapeño and cheddar.

Pour the batter into the prepared muffin tin, filling each cup about halfway. Bake for 13 to 17 minutes until a toothpick stuck in the center of a muffin comes out mostly clean. Don't overbake.

Serve warm with butter and Homemade Jalapeño Jam.

Makes 12 muffins

½ cup (66 g) coarse-ground yellow cornmeal

½ cup (63 g) all-purpose flour

¼ cup (50 g) sugar

¼ teaspoon kosher salt

¼ teaspoon baking soda

1 egg, beaten

½ cup (120 g) buttermilk

½ cup (112 g, or 1 stick) unsalted butter, melted, plus more softened butter to serve

1 jalapeño, stemmed, seeded, and finely diced

2 ounces (55 g) aged cheddar (I prefer Tillamook), grated (approximately ½ cup)

Homemade Jalapeño Jam (recipe follows)

HOMEMADE JALAPEÑO JAM

7 fresh jalapeños, stemmed, seeded, and finely diced

4 pickled red cherry peppers, finely diced

½ cup (120 ml) liquid from the cherry pepper jar

1½ cups (355 ml) white wine vinegar

¾ cup (150 g) sugar

1½ teaspoons kosher salt

½ cup (160 g) apricot preserves

This quick recipe for jalapeño pepper jam is a team favorite as many grew up eating some variation of it. We like to drizzle it on top of our Cheesy "Hushpuppies" and slather it on warm cornbread muffins with softened butter. This jam will be your jam soon!

Combine the jalapeños and red cherry peppers in medium saucepan and add the liquid from cherry peppers, the white wine vinegar, sugar, and salt. Heat over medium heat and let simmer until the mixture is almost dry and a shiny glaze forms, 5 to 7 minutes.

Remove from the heat and fold in the apricot preserves until combined. Transfer the jam to a clean jar with a lid and refrigerate for up to three weeks.

Makes 2 cups (608 g)

ROOTS & FRUITS

I fell in love with the name of this salad before I fell in love with the taste . . . insane! Our Char Bar chef, Mark Kelpe, invented it. He calls it, "A kaleidoscope of color packing an umami punch of flavor. It has earthy bitterness from the beets and parsnips, sweetness from the oranges, a sour tang from the goat cheese, and a salty crunch from the pistachios." Yum. Although this sweet and savory veggie salad can be served anytime of the year, it really shines in fall and winter—whenever beets are in season in your area.

2 red beets

2 gold beets

2 parsnips

12 brussels sprouts

½ yellow onion

¼ cup (60 ml) extra virgin olive oil

1 teaspoon kosher salt

½ teaspoon freshly ground black pepper

1 cup (235 ml) Blackberry Vinaigrette (recipe follows)

12 fresh orange segments

2 ounces (55 g) fresh goat cheese

3 tablespoons (23 g) toasted pistachios

Preheat the oven to 375°F (190°C, or gas mark 5). Line a large baking sheet with aluminum foil.

Peel and dice the red and gold beets into ½-inch (1 cm) cubes. Peel and slice the parsnips in half lengthwise and then into ½-inch (1 cm) half-moons. Slice the Brussels sprouts into quarters. Slice the yellow onion into ¼-inch (6 mm) cubes. Toss the vegetables with the olive oil, kosher salt, and black pepper. Spread the cut vegetables out evenly into a single layer on the prepared baking sheet.

Roast for 18 to 22 minutes until the beets can be easily pierced with a tip of a paring knife. Cool to room temperature or refrigerate if making ahead.

To assemble the salad, in large mixing bowl, toss the roasted vegetables with the Blackberry Vinaigrette to coat. Arrange the vegetables on a platter with the orange segments. Crumble goat cheese over the salad and garnish with toasted pistachios.

Serves 4 as a main dish

BLACKBERRY VINAIGRETTE

1 cup (145 g) fresh blackberries (frozen berries will work in a pinch)

½ shallot, finely diced

½ cup (120 ml) red wine vinegar

1 tablespoon (15 ml) Tabasco chipotle pepper sauce

¼ cup (50 g) sugar

½ teaspoon crushed red pepper flakes

¾ teaspoon kosher salt

1 cup (235 ml) canola oil

Combine the blackberries, shallot, vinegar, Tabasco, sugar, red pepper, and salt in blender. Purée until combined. With the motor running, slowly drizzle in canola oil. Use immediately or refrigerate for up to 1 week.

Makes 2 cups (475 ml)

CHARRED SALMON BLT

At Char Bar, we quickly found that not everyone wants beef, chicken, and pork every day. Weird, right? Anyhow, our corporate chef, Michael Peterson, created this sandwich, which has become an excellent alternative and works well when heirloom tomatoes are in season. Michael is super passionate about getting local heirlooms from Kurlbaum Farms and prefers using wild-caught salmon. Wild-caught salmon has a richer flavor due to its high-fat content, while a farm-raised salmon will be mellower in taste. As in any protein, higher fat means a more buttery bite.

To cook the bacon, line a large rimmed baking sheet with aluminum foil. Arrange the bacon slices in a single layer on the baking sheet, with no overlapping. Turn on the oven to 400°F (200°C, or gas mark 6), with a rack in the middle of the oven. Don't wait for the oven to preheat; place the baking sheet on the middle rack and cook for 12 to 17 minutes until the bacon is done to your preferred crispness. The timing will vary depending on how thick the bacon was cut, so start checking at 10 minutes, when you begin to smell that sweet aroma. Remove the bacon from the oven and transfer to a platter lined with paper towels.

To prepare the salmon, pat the fillets with a paper towel until dry. Season with the rub and spray each side with the cooking spray or a neutral-tasting oil.

To prepare the grill, start with a clean grill and preheat on high (450 to 500°F [230 to 250°C]) with the lid closed for 15 minutes. Lightly soak a paper towel in vegetable oil, wrap the soaked towel around a pair on barbecue tongs, and quickly rub the hot grill grates to season them and prevent sticking. To grill the salmon, reduce the grill heat to medium. Place the fillets on the seasoned grill grates and cook, uncovered, gently flipping with a flat spatula after 6 minutes. The sugar from the barbecue rub will begin to char the exterior of the fish. When the center of the fillets reaches 120°F (49°C) on an instant-read thermometer, transfer the fish to a platter, loosely cover with foil, and let it rest a few minutes to allow for carryover cooking.

To start assembling the sandwiches while the salmon is resting, brush the potato buns with melted butter and place on grill to toast for 30 seconds until golden. Spread each toasted bottom bun with 1 tablespoon (15 g) of the Barbecue Ranch sauce. Season the tomato slices with a pinch each of salt and pepper. Layer each bun with a cold iceberg lettuce leaf, large tomato slice, two slices of crisp bacon, and the charred salmon fillet. Top with the bun and serve.

TIP: To determine the grill temperature, hold your hand 3 to 4 inches (7.5 to 10 cm) above the grill grates. When you can hold your hand in place for no more than three "one–one thousand" counts, the grill is the right temperature to start grilling.

Serves 4

8 slices thick-cut bacon

4 skinless salmon fillets (6 to 8 ounces, or 170 to 225 g each)

¼ cup (24 g) Meat Mitch All-Purpose Rub (see page 28)

Nonstick cooking spray or neutral oil

¼ cup (60 g) Barbecue Ranch (see page 77)

4 potato buns (I prefer Martin's)

¼ cup (56 g, or ½ stick) unsalted butter, melted

4 large slices ripe tomato

Kosher salt and freshly ground black pepper

4 large leaves iceberg lettuce

KALE PARMESAN SLAW

Our team came up with this healthy, modern alternative to the usual line-up of barbecue sides. (Lord knows I didn't invent it!) Still, this quickly became a house favorite and go-to side. A couple of quick tips: First, you can leave out the grated Parmesan cheese to make this side dish completely vegan. Second, the Lemon Vinaigrette used to dress this slaw is also fantastic drizzled over grilled fish.

2 pounds (900 g) lacinato kale (10 to 12 large leaves)

1 cup (235 ml) Lemon Vinaigrette (recipe follows)

½ cup (50 g) freshly grated Parmesan cheese

½ cup (60 g) homemade breadcrumbs (recipe follows)

½ teaspoon kosher salt

¼ teaspoon freshly ground black pepper

Remove any large stems from the bottom of the kale stalks. Place several leaves on top of one another and roll together; then, slice the bundle into ¼ inch (6 mm)-wide strips. Repeat with the remaining kale.

Combine 4 quarts (3.8 L) of water and 1 tablespoon (15 g) of kosher salt in large stockpot and bring to a rapid boil. Place 2 quarts (1.9 L) of water with 1 quart (1.9 L) of ice in large mixing bowl and stir. With a skimmer handy, add all the kale to the boiling water; stir once around and quickly transfer the kale to the ice bath. Drain well, removing any remaining ice cubes. Transfer the kale to a kitchen towel and roll up, gently pressing to remove any water.

Gently toss the kale in a mixing bowl with the vinaigrette, 6 tablespoons (30 g) of the Parmesan cheese, 6 tablespoons (42 g) of the breadcrumbs, salt, and pepper. Transfer the kale to serving bowl. Garnish with remaining 2 tablespoons (10 g) of grated Parmesan cheese and 2 tablespoons (14 g) of breadcrumbs.

TIP: You can also add toasted walnuts or almonds, if you wish.

Serves 8 as a side

LEMON VINAIGRETTE

½ shallot, finely diced

¼ cup (60 ml) aged white wine vinegar

2 tablespoons (28 ml) freshly squeezed lemon juice

2 tablespoons (26 g) sugar

½ cup (120 ml) extra virgin olive oil

½ teaspoon kosher salt

¼ teaspoon freshly ground black pepper

Combine the shallot, white wine vinegar, lemon juice, and sugar in mixing bowl, whisking to combine. Slowly add the olive oil, while whisking vigorously, until all of the oil is incorporated. Season with salt and black pepper to taste.

Makes 1 cup (235 ml)

HOMEMADE BREADCRUMBS

4 cups (200 g) chopped or torn bread, preferably leftover

6 tablespoons (105 ml) extra virgin olive oil

¼ teaspoon kosher salt

¼ teaspoon garlic powder

This is a great use for all those trimmed bread crusts that are left over after making our Peach Bread Pudding (page 101).

Preheat the oven to 400°F (200°C, or gas mark 6).

Put the bread in a mixing bowl. Add the remaining ingredients and toss to make sure all the pieces of bread are well coated. Transfer to a baking sheet, spread out in a single layer, and bake in for 8 to 12 minutes until golden brown. Let cool.

Put the cooled bread into a zip top storage bag and use a rolling pin to crush into a coarse consistency. Use immediately or keep for up to 4 weeks in a tightly sealed container at room temperature.

Makes ½ cup (60 g)

SPICY COLESLAW

This slaw is nontraditional, but so delicious you might just make it your new house slaw. It's crisp and tangy with a sneaky hint of heat from the Sriracha balanced by the cooling buttermilk. It's the kind of recipe that makes my tongue do push-ups!

Cut the cabbage into quarters and remove the core. Slice the cabbage quarters into thin shreds and then dice into ¼-inch (6 mm) chunks.

In a large mixing bowl, combine the cabbage, carrot, shallot, and parsley.

In a separate mixing bowl, combine the mayonnaise, buttermilk, mustard, cider vinegar, lemon juice, sugar, Sriracha, salt, pepper, and celery seeds; mix well. Transfer the slaw dressing to the chopped cabbage mix and toss by hand until thoroughly combined.

Refrigerate for at least 1 hour and toss again before serving. Store leftovers covered in the refrigerator for up to 2 days.

Serves about 10

1 medium cabbage (about 2 pounds, or 900 g), outer leaves removed

1 medium carrot, peeled and shredded with a box grater

1 shallot, finely diced

½ cup (30 g) coarsely chopped and loosely packed flat-leaf parsley

¾ cup (240 g) mayonnaise (I prefer Duke's)

½ cup (120 ml) buttermilk

1 tablespoon (15 g) Dijon mustard

3 tablespoons (45 ml) cider vinegar

¼ cup (60 ml) freshly squeezed lemon juice

½ cup (100 g) sugar

1 teaspoon Sriracha hot sauce

1 teaspoon kosher salt

½ teaspoon freshly ground black pepper

½ teaspoon celery seeds

"PIG-TAIL" MAC 'N' CHEESE

Mac and cheese has become ubiquitous on restaurant menus these days. We set ours apart by using a hollow corkscrew-shaped pasta, called cavatappi, that sorta resembles a curly pig's tail. Variations can be endless—add smoked bacon, peas, or caramelized onion or even top it with chunky, charred pieces of burnt ends. Heck, you may want to take a dip in it yourself, it's so good!

In large stockpot, bring 4 quarts (3.8 L) of water to a rolling boil. Stir in 1 tablespoon (15 g) of kosher salt. Add the pasta and cook, stirring occasionally, until al dente. Drain the pasta and set aside in large mixing bowl.

Preheat oven to 350°F (180°, or gas mark 4). Butter a 9- by 13-inch (23 by 33 cm) baking dish.

In a medium saucepan, melt 2 tablespoons (28 g) of the butter over medium heat. Add 2 tablespoons (16 g) the flour and cook for 5 minutes, whisking constantly to form a roux. Remove the pan from the heat. Add the heavy cream and whole milk, whisking until the roux dissolves. Return the pan to medium-high heat and continue stirring until the liquid begins to thicken. Remove from the heat. Stir in the Velveeta and Parmesan cheese. Add the kosher salt and black pepper.

Fold the warm cheese sauce into the cooked pasta until combined. Transfer the pasta to the prepared baking dish. Top with the Buttered Parmesan Breadcrumbs.

Bake for 18 to 20 minutes until the pasta is heated throughout and the breadcrumbs are golden brown. Serve hot.

TIP: If you like, top the mac and cheese with burnt ends (see Competition-Style Beef Brisket and Burnt Ends, page 57) or Pig Candy (see page 165).

Serves about 8 as a side

- 1 pound (455 g) cavatappi pasta
- 8 tablespoons (1 stick, or 112 g) unsalted butter, at room temperature
- 2 tablespoons (16 g) all-purpose flour
- 1½ cups (355 ml) heavy cream
- 1½ cups (355 g) whole milk
- 1¼ pounds (570 g) Velveeta cheese, shredded
- 2 tablespoons (10 g) freshly grated Parmesan cheese
- 1 teaspoon kosher salt
- ¼ teaspoon freshly ground black pepper
- ½ cup (47 g) Buttered Parmesan Breadcrumbs (recipe on page 98)

BUTTERED PARMESAN BREADCRUMBS

for "PIG-TAIL" MAC 'N' CHEESE

½ cup (56 g) panko breadcrumbs

2 tablespoons (10 g) freshly grated Parmesan cheese

2 tablespoons (28 g) unsalted butter, melted

Combine the panko breadcrumbs, Parmesan cheese, and melted butter in small mixing bowl. Toss to combine.

Makes about ½ cup (47 g)

JALAPEÑO CHEESY-CORN BAKE

While Fiorella's Jack Stack Barbecue is credited with the original version of Cheesy Corn, our corporate chef, Michael Peterson, set out to create a more flavorful, cheesier version of Kansas City's iconic side dish. At Char Bar, we use a colorful jalapeño sofrito (a sofrito is a mix of sautéed peppers, onion, and garlic, at the heart of many Latin American and Spanish recipes) to bump up the heat. We also grill fresh ears of sweet corn over live hickory wood for maximum flavor—of course we do! In a pinch, you can use frozen corn kernels (like the original), and it will still yield a great result; however, we feel our version "stacks" up above the rest.

Preheat a gas grill to high (450 to 500°F [230 to 250°C]) and heat for 10 minutes, or prepare a hot fire in a charcoal grill. Lightly brush the corn with the vegetable oil and sprinkle with the smoked paprika and 1 teaspoon of the salt.

Place the corn on the grill and cook, turning often, until charred all over, about 10 minutes. Remove from the grill and let cool slightly. Using a knife, shave the kernels off of the cob into a bowl. Add the prepared Jalapeño Sofrito to the corn kernels and mix to combine. Set aside.

To make the Jalapeño Sofrito, heat the vegetable oil in medium sauté pan over medium heat for 1 minute until the oil is hot. Add the jalapeño, red and green peppers, shallot, garlic, and kosher salt. Do not stir the peppers and shallot for the first minute until slight color begins to form. Continue to sauté over medium heat, stirring occasionally, until the peppers soften and the diced shallot becomes translucent. Remove from the heat.

Preheat the oven to 375°F (190°C, or gas mark 5). Butter an 8-inch (20 cm) square baking dish.

Heat the milk in large saucepan over medium heat until it just barely reaches a simmer. Do not scald the milk. Add the shredded Velveeta. Remove from the heat and stir until smooth and creamy. Fold in the corn. Fold in the sofrito and season with the remaining ½ teaspoon of salt and black pepper. Transfer the cheesy corn into the prepared baking dish. Top with the Homemade Breadcrumbs.

Bake for 20 to 25 minutes until the casserole is golden brown and bubbly. Serve hot.

Serves 4 to 6 as a side

6 medium ears of fresh sweet corn, husked; or 2 pounds (900 g) frozen kernels, thawed

¼ cup (60 ml) vegetable oil

1 teaspoon smoked paprika

1½ teaspoons kosher salt

1 cup (310 g) Jalapeño Sofrito (recipe follows)

½ cup (120 ml) whole milk

1¼ pounds (570 g) Velveeta cheese, shredded

¼ teaspoon freshly ground black pepper

2 tablespoons (28 g) unsalted butter, at room temperature

½ cup (60 g) Homemade Breadcrumbs (see page 94)

Jalepeño Sofrito:

2 tablespoons (28 ml) vegetable oil

1 small jalapeño, stemmed, seeded, and finely diced

½ green bell pepper, stemmed, seeded, and finely diced

½ red bell pepper, stemmed, seeded, and finely diced

1 medium shallot, finely diced

1 garlic clove, minced

½ teaspoon kosher salt

PEACH BREAD PUDDING WITH CARAMEL SAUCE

The quintessential Southern crowd-pleasing dessert has always been a giant pan of warm peach bread pudding. Our version includes a golden-brown caramel sauce to drizzle over the top before serving.

Preheat the oven to 350°F (180°C, or gas mark 4).

Remove the crusts from the sliced bread and discard or save to make Homemade Breadcrumbs (see page 94). Dice the bread into ½-inch (13 mm) cubes. Spread the bread cubes on a sheet pan and toast in oven for 12 minutes until slightly golden brown.

Divide the peaches in half. Place 1½ pounds (680 g) of the peaches in a food processor and purée until smooth.

In large mixing bowl, combine the puréed peaches, heavy cream, eggs, the white sugar, salt, cinnamon, and vanilla. Gently fold the toasted bread cubes into the cream mixture. Set aside for at least 15 minutes and up to 1 hour.

Dice the remaining peaches into ½-inch (13 mm) cubes and put in medium mixing bowl. Sprinkle the cubed peaches with ½ cup (96 g) of the turbinado sugar until combined. Set aside.

Brush the insides of a 9- by 13-inch (23 by 33 cm) baking dish with the softened butter. Sprinkle the remaining ½ cup (96 g) of turbinado sugar on the inside of the baking dish. Transfer the soaked bread cubes into the baking dish, drain the peaches and discard the juice, and evenly distribute the diced peaches on top.

Loosely cover the baking dish with foil and bake for 20 minutes. Remove the foil and bake for 20 to 25 minutes longer until the top is golden and the center is set.

Remove from the oven and let rest for at least 15 minutes. Drizzle with the Caramel Sauce and serve with fresh whipped cream or vanilla bean ice cream.

Serves 6 to 8 average people or three hungry pitmasters named Jimbo

1 loaf thick-sliced white bread or Texas toast (about 24 ounces, or 680 g)

3 pounds (1.4 kg) frozen peaches, thawed

2 cups (475 ml) heavy cream

6 eggs

¾ cup (150 g) white sugar

1 teaspoon kosher salt

½ teaspoon ground cinnamon

1½ teaspoons vanilla extract

1 cup (192 g) turbinado sugar (I prefer Sugar in the Raw)

3 tablespoons (42 g) unsalted butter, at room temperature

Caramel Sauce (recipe follows)

Whipped cream or vanilla bean ice cream, to serve

CARAMEL SAUCE

1 cup (2 sticks, or 225 g) unsalted butter

1 cup (235 ml) heavy cream

1 packed (225 g) cup light brown sugar

In a heavy saucepan, stir together the butter, heavy cream, and brown sugar over medium heat until it reaches a boil. Reduce the heat to low and continue to simmer until the sauce thickens, about 5 minutes. Use warm. Extra sauce can be refrigerated for up to 2 weeks.

Makes about 3 cups (960 g)

BURNT BUTTERSCOTCH CUSTARD

We wanted to create our own take on the classic French crème brûlée by caramelizing two sugars to create a nutty butterscotch flavor. This is a fun dessert to make for those who are fond of using a blowtorch in the kitchen—which should be everyone!

2 tablespoons (28 g) unsalted butter

¼ cup (50 g) granulated white sugar

¼ packed (60 g) cup light brown sugar

2 cups (475 ml) heavy cream

5 egg yolks

½ teaspoon vanilla extract

4 teaspoons (16 g) superfine sugar

Preheat the oven to 325°F (170°C, or gas mark 3).

In a medium stainless saucepan, melt the butter over medium-high heat. Add the white and brown sugars and stir constantly with a high-heat spatula until the sugars begin to caramelize and give off a nutty aroma. Watch carefully because the sugar will caramelize very quickly. Remove from the heat.

Add the cream while whisking. Set aside.

In small mixing bowl, beat the egg yolks. Gradually add the hot cream mixture to the egg yolks, ¼ cup (60 ml) at a time, until the yolk mixture is tempered. Stir in the vanilla.

Pour the custard into four 6-ounce (175 ml) ramekins and place the ramekins in a baking dish; fill the baking dish with boiling water to come halfway up the sides of the ramekins.

Bake for 30 to 40 minutes until the centers are barely set. Cool completely.

Refrigerate for at least several hours or up to a couple of days.

When you're ready to serve, top each custard with about a teaspoon of superfine sugar in a thin layer. Using a kitchen blowtorch, caramelize the sugar layer until the sugar melts and browns or even blackens a bit. Serve immediately.

Serves 4

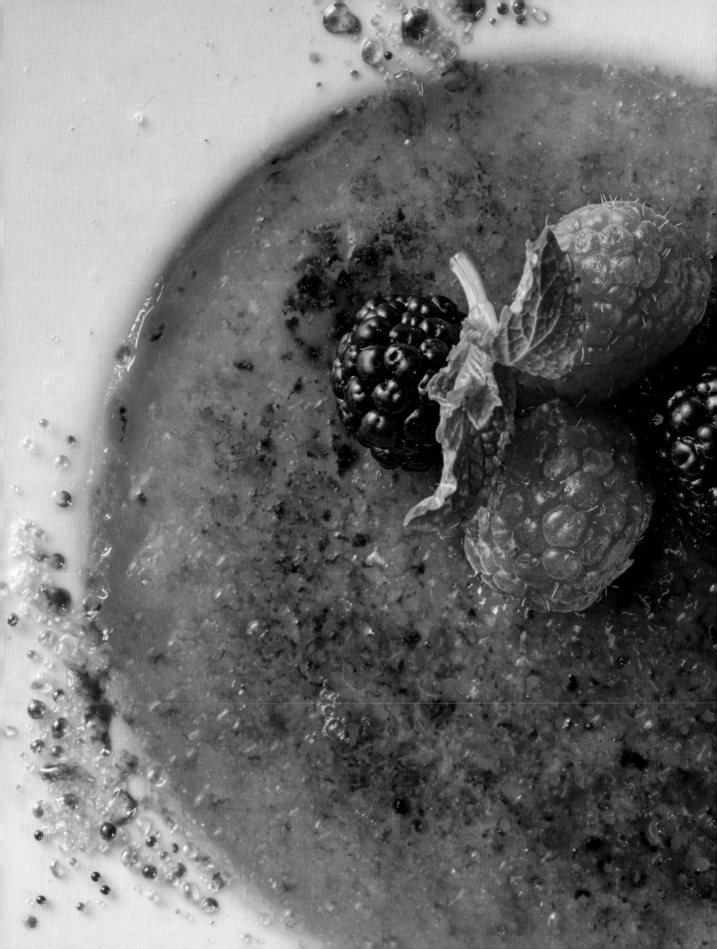

JESS PRYLES

HARDCORE CARNIVORE
AUSTIN, TEXAS

Oh the glory of social media! I found Jess Pryles several years ago through Instagram under the name Burger Mary. She had tons of great barbecue content and a kick-ass Australian accent, so I sent her samples of my sauces and rubs to try. Fortunately for me, she liked them enough to help me by recommending them to her followers! We kept in touch and it wasn't too long before she reached out to let me know she was coming to Kansas City for a residency to train and become a certified barbecue chef. I volunteered to take her around town and introduce her to folks at some of my favorite Kansas City restaurants. A great friendship was forged!

The Meat Mitch team and I have hosted Jess for several years now when she travels to Kansas City for the The American Royal World Series of Barbecue, and we also try to hang out every year at the Memphis in May World Championship Barbecue Cooking Contest. We have had fun trips to New Orleans for Hogs for the Cause BBQ Competition, and she was kind enough to feature me as a guest chef at her famous Carnivores Ball held in Austin, Texas. She gave me the honor of cooking alongside Wayne Mueller from Louie Muller BBQ and pitmaster Evan LeRoy and served my food to the legendary greats like Chris Lilly from Big Bob Gibson Bar-B-Q in Decatur, Alabama, and Billy Durney from Hometown Bar-B-Q in Brooklyn, New York.

Jess never ceases to amaze me with her relentless pursuit of knowledge. She has transformed her brand from Burger Mary into the worldwide barbecue phenomenon, Hardcore Carnivore. She is now a United States citizen and a screamin' proud adopted Texan. Jess is a cookbook author, meat science expert, pitmaster, product innovator, sales person, and marketing extraordinaire, but most importantly, she's my buddy. Hai, Pods! (That's "Hi, Pods!" with Jess's accent . . . see page 32 if you're confused!)

SMOKED TRI TIP STEAK

RECIPE BY JESS PRYLES

Tri tip has become very popular everywhere I look. It's generally a little less expensive than most steaks but delivers all the flavor you can handle. It was first introduced to me by my competition friends on the West Coast. It is usually cooked over direct heat on the grill, but it's actually awesome on the smoker. Tri tip cooks to perfection in about an hour, but the key is to use the Jess's Hardcore Carnivore Black seasoning, which gives you a great bark even with the short cook time. Don't forget to cut against the grain!

2½-pound (1.1 kg) beef tri tip steak

2 tablespoons (35 g) Hardcore Carnivore Black Beef Seasoning (see Tips below)

Set your smoker at 250°F (120°C) and get a good smoke rolling.

Let's butcher this steak. We want to take a boning or filet knife and trim off any of the silverskin and membrane from the outside of the steak. Silverskin doesn't break down or render on the smoker, so if you don't take it off, your tender smoked meat will seem tough as an old shoe.

Rub the Hardcore Carnivore Black Beef Seasoning all over the trimmed beef and then place in the smoker. Insert your trusty probe thermometer into the thickest part of the beef. We want to smoke our tri tip for about 1½ hours or until it reaches 130°F (54.5°C) internally. Once it gets to temperature, take it out of the smoker and wrap it in aluminum foil or butcher paper to rest for 30 minutes.

When it's time to serve, clean your sharpest knife and make sure to slice thinly against the grain. It's time to eat!

TIPS: You can buy Jess's Hardcore Carnivore Black Beef Seasoning on her website at jesspryles.com or on Amazon. Try the steak paired with Jess's Smoked Garlic Sauce on page 109.

Serves 4 to 6

SMOKED GARLIC SAUCE

RECIPE BY JESS PRYLES

This smoked garlic sauce packs a ton of flavor but is also mellow and delicate. The garlic develops a smoky sweetness and pairs beautifully with smoked lamb or chicken.

Cut the tops off the garlic bulbs to just see the cloves inside. Place in a microwave-safe container with 2 tablespoons (28 ml) of water at the bottom. Cover and microwave on medium power for 5 to 6 minutes to steam the garlic and make it nice and tender.

Set a smoker to 300°F (150°C) and get a good smoke rolling. Create three shallow "boats" of foil or one large "boat" and place the garlic bulbs inside. Smoke for 20 to 25 minutes until the cloves are completely soft.

Once cooked, squeeze the garlic cloves out from the papery skin and place into a food processor or blender. Pulse several times until smooth.

Add in the mayonnaise, sour cream, lemon juice, and vinegar. Pulse again to combine and add salt to taste.

TIP: If you don't want to use a smoker for this, you can use a gas or charcoal grill. Throw a handful of woodchips onto the coals and then place garlic on the grill. Close the lid and cook for 20 to 25 minutes until the garlic is completely soft.

Makes 1 heaping cup (240 g) of smoky goodness

3 whole garlic bulbs

2 tablespoons (28 ml) water

½ cup (115 g) mayonnaise (I prefer Duke's)

¼ cup (60 g) sour cream

2 tablespoons (28 ml) freshly squeezed lemon juice

2 tablespoons (28 ml) apple cider vinegar

Kosher salt

3

REVOLUTIONARY BBQ: THINKING OUTSIDE THE SMOKE BOX

Whether you are plodding through everyday life or navigating through crazy, unprecedented times, one thing remains consistent: everyone loves great barbecue! While barbecue may be one of the oldest methods of cooking—I am harkening back to cavemen cooking over live fire a million years ago—it is also continually reinvented. From reverse searing to sous vide, barbecue is modernizing and evolving . . . and so can you!

In this chapter, we'll explore different ways to prepare your favorite meats as well as dive into some lesser-smoked proteins from shellfish to jackfruit. We'll look deep into the ribeye and learn a different way to prepare mom's meatloaf. Follow me and you'll never spell the classic b-o-l-o-g-n-a sandwich the same way again—and you may also find that adding tequila to chili makes it so you can't spell anything at all!

Don't worry. I'm not saying you should ever replace traditional barbecue. I'm just giving you the license to have some fun and find some new ways to make people smile. Let's get started!

SMOKED BRISKET SMASH BURGERS

Step right up for thin griddled patties with cheese that double up your pleasure with charred bits of love and crusty crunches of something that surely should be illegal. Note that this recipe is scaled for party, but you can halve it for five burgers—enough for a family of four plus an extra for the chef.

In a large mixing bowl or in an electric stand mixer, gently mix the beef chuck and the chopped brisket. Don't overmix this or the burgers will get pasty and not have the texture we are going for here, Pods. If you have a scale (get one), measure out the burger mix into four-ounce (115 g) balls.

Set your burger balls aside and get a griddle pan hot. Set out a baking sheet lined with a wire rack. When the pan is rippin' hot, season the outside of the burger balls with some Meat Mitch Steer Season Rub, saving enough for the backside of the burgers.

Place half of the burger balls, seasoned-side down, on the griddle, making sure not to overcrowd. Now comes the best part—smash time! Using the back of a metal spatula, press down on the burger balls until they are flat—get them flat! Try to do it in one single smash per ball. They should be frayed on the edges. This is the best part that gets nice and crispy on the exterior.

Season the top of the patties with more Meat Mitch Steer Season Rub. Cook for 1 to 2 minutes, depending on the quality of your smash. Flip and immediately place the cheese on the burgers. Cook just until the cheese begins to melt and then slide the burgers onto the wire rack set over the baking sheet.

Repeat with the remaining burgers and serve on toasted potato buns with any toppings and condiments on the side.

TIP: While I recommend a griddle for this recipe if you have one, a ripping hot cast iron pan can also work.

Makes 10 double burgers, the only way to party

3½ pounds (1.6 kg) ground chuck (preferably 80 percent lean)

1½ pounds (680 g) chopped leftover Competition-Style Beef Brisket and Burnt Ends (see page 57)

3 tablespoons (53 g) Meat Mitch Steer Season Rub, store-bought or homemade (see page 31)

20 slices American cheese

10 potato buns or any burger bun you love (I love Martin's), toasted

Any toppings and condiments you want

REVERSE SMOKED TOMAHAWK RIBEYE

People have been cooking great steak for a million years, and now here I am trying to tell you there might be a new, better way . . . you'll just have to try and see for yourself. Reverse searing is the process of cooking meat slowly and evenly before finishing it with a sear. Most cooks do the first part in the oven, but I create the same effect on the smoker to give it extra flavor. Once the cut reaches the desired internal temperature (doneness), I like to finish it off over a ripping hot grill to create a beautiful crust.

2½-pound (1.1 kg) tomahawk ribeye steak, cut no less than 2 inches (5 cm) thick by your butcher

2 tablespoons (33 g) Meat Mitch Steer Season Rub, store-bought or homemade (see page 31)

½ cup (140 g) Meat Mitch Competition WHOMP! BBQ Sauce, store-bought or homemade, (see page 32) (optional)

One hour before cooking, fire up the smoker to 225°F (107°C) and get a good smoke rolling. Remove the steak from the refrigerator and season all over with the Meat Mitch Steer Season Rub. Allow the steak to come to room temperature and allow the spices start to work their magic.

When the smoker is rolling, add the steak and insert a digital probe meat thermometer. Keep an eye on the thermometer as all steaks cook a little differently, but you can plan on smoking for about 1 hour.

Toward the end of the smoking time, fire up a gas or charcoal grill as hot as it will go (450 to 500°F [230 to 250°C]). (If you don't have a grill, you can place a grate over top of the firebox.)

For a medium-rare steak (my favorite), remove the steak from the smoker when the internal temperature reaches 125°F (52°C). For medium, remove at 135°F (57°C). For medium-well or above . . . I couldn't bring myself to even test a beautiful steak. Using metal grill tongs, place the steak on a grill or the grate on your smoker to create the crust. It should take about 1 minute per side.

Rest the steak for 5 to 10 minutes. With this technique, the rest is not essential, but I say give that baby time to bloom. Slice perpendicularly to your cutting board, starting at the curved end of the steak and working towards the bone. (Don't give the bone to the dog, go hide in a corner and gnaw on it yourself.) Serve.

TIP: For a revolutionary barbecue alternative, using a pastry brush, glaze the meat with Meat Mitch Competition WHOMP! BBQ Sauce (see page 32) after smoking. Use your tongs and flip often over the coals until lightly charred all over, being careful not to let the sugars in the sauce burn. With most recipes, I only like to flip once, but in this case, I'm flipping like Simone Biles.

Serves 2 to 4, depending on what else you are serving

SMOKED AND BBQ-GLAZED MEATLOAF

Meatloaf reminds me of my Dad—he loved it and so I grew up on it. For me, the best way to enjoy meatloaf is having a leftover slice sandwiched between white bread with mayonnaise the next day . . . still today one of my favorite sandwiches of all time. Okay, let me tell you about my meatloaf: I combine beef and pork sausage and my Meat Mitch Steer Season Rub as the base, and it's glazed with my Meat Mitch Competition WHOMP! BBQ Sauce. Since it's smoked as well, it takes your traditional meatloaf to another level. If only my Dad could have tried this on a sandwich.

Set your smoker to 260°F (127°C) and get a good smoke rolling. We want to hit this with a lot of smoke, so get smaller pieces or chips ready once the fire is ready. Line a cookie sheet with parchment paper.

In a sauté pan over medium-high heat, melt the bacon drippings. Add the onion and cook, stirring frequently, until soft and translucent, about 5 minutes. Add the garlic and cook for 2 more minutes. Remove from the heat and set aside.

In a large mixing bowl, combine the breadcrumbs and milk. Let the breadcrumbs soak for 15 minutes until a soggy mess forms in the bottom of the bowl. Whisk in the eggs, salt, and pepper. Add the parsley, beef, pork, and cheddar and mix by hand, just enough to bring all of the ingredients together. Mound the meat mix on the prepared baking sheet. Form into a log shape. Season the loaf with the Meat Mitch Steer Season Rub and place in the smoker. A probe thermometer makes cooking a meatloaf super easy, so if you have one, insert the probe into the middle of the loaf and set the alarm to go off when the internal temperature hits 160°F (71°C), which will take about 2 hours. Close the lid and grab a beer. After 1½ hours, generously apply the Meat Mitch Competition WHOMP! BBQ Sauce on top and spread all over with a pastry brush or a spoon. Let the sauce glaze over for the last 30 minutes of cooking.

Remove the meatloaf from the smoker and let rest for about 20 minutes. Slice and serve with extra sauce on the side.

Serves 6 hungry friends

1 yellow onion, minced

3 cloves garlic, minced

3 tablespoons (45 g) leftover bacon drippings, unsalted butter, or (45 ml) any vegetable oil

1 cup (115 g) dried breadcrumbs

¾ cup (175 ml) whole milk

3 large eggs, lightly beaten

1 tablespoon (15 g) kosher salt

2 teaspoons freshly ground black pepper

¼ cup (15 g) finely chopped flat-leaf parsley

2 pounds (900 g) ground beef (preferably 80 percent lean)

1 pound (455 g) raw pork sausage or ground pork

2 cups (225 g) shredded sharp cheddar cheese

½ cup (96 g) Meat Mitch Steer Season Rub, store-bought or homemade (see page 31)

1 cup (280 g) Meat Mitch Competition WHOMP! BBQ Sauce, store-bought or homemade (see page 32), plus extra to serve

TEQUILA TWO-STEP TEXAS CHILI

This recipe is the result of years of chili recipe testing. In it, I have gathered my favorite ingredients and created something all my own: I call it MITCHili at home! Texas-style chilis don't have any beans—but they do have plenty of meat. With three types of meat, beer, and tequila, it eats like a great party. But the booze isn't just for the fun factor, it adds complexity. And don't worry, you won't need a bouncer for this party because the alcohol will cook off. (For those who want a quick version of this: just eat the cooked bacon and shoot the tequila . . . I won't tell a soul and just might join you.)

You'll notice that this recipe is broken up into 2 separate steps. This is the format that is required when preparing chili for a competition.

STEP 1

1 pound (455 g) bacon, cut into ½-inch (13 mm) matchsticks

4 large garlic cloves, minced

2 white onions, diced

3 tablespoons (23 g) canned diced green chiles

2¼ cups (535 ml) beef broth

1½ teaspoons granulated garlic

1½ teaspoons granulated onion

STEP 2

1½ cups (355 ml) beef broth

1 can (28 ounces, or 785 g) diced tomatoes

¼ cup (30 g) chili powder

3 tablespoons (21 g) ground cumin

1½ teaspoons dried oregano

1½ teaspoons sweet paprika

1 tablespoon (15 g) kosher salt

1 bottle (12 ounce, or 355 ml) wheat beer

2 ounces (60 ml) tequila

1 pound (455 g) smoked pork butt (see Competition-Style Pulled Pork, page 51), cooled and diced small

1 pound (455 g) smoked brisket scraps (see Competition-Style Beef Brisket and Burnt Ends, page 57), cooled and diced small

Assorted garnishes, such as chopped raw white onion, shredded cheddar cheese, pickled jalapeños, sour cream, and oyster crackers

FOR STEP 1, in a large stockpot, render the bacon until crispy. Remove the bacon with a large slotted spoon and drain most of the bacon grease into a container for later use. Sauté the onion and garlic over medium heat in the remaining bacon grease left in the pot for 15 minutes until the onions are soft and translucent.

Add the green chiles, broth, granulated garlic, and granulated onion. Bring to a boil and then turn down to a simmer. Simmer for 45 minutes, covered, to ensure that the onions are soft.

FOR STEP 2, add the remaining 1½ cups (355 ml) of beef broth, the tomatoes, chili powder, cumin, oregano, paprika, salt, beer, and tequila and stir. Bring to a boil and then turn down to a simmer. Simmer for 20 minutes or until slightly thickened.

Add the smoked pork, brisket, and bacon and simmer for another 10 minutes. Once thickened to a desired consistency, ladle into bowls and serve with all of your favorite garnishes.

Serves 8

SMOKED MORTADELLA SANDWICH

I found this baby at Au Cheval, a restaurant in Chicago near my buddies' condo in the West Loop. It's a small, insanely amazing restaurant that pumps out great food and drink. This is my riff on their classic sandwich. Note that this recipe makes more mortadella than you need for four sandwiches, but it's better to have more than enough—just in case the neighbors find out what you are up to. Crisping the thinly sliced mortadella in a cast iron pan, on a flat top, or even charring on the grill is key to getting the texture necessary for this king of all sandwiches.

To make the aioli, whisk together the egg yolks, lemon juice, and mustard in a small bowl. Mix together the olive and canola oils and slowly pour into the yolk mixture in a constant stream, continually whisking, until all the oil is incorporated and the mixture is thick and emulsified. Whisk in the garlic and season with salt and pepper. Cover and place in the refrigerator until you are ready to make the sandwiches. (Store any leftover in the refrigerator for up to 1 week.)

To make the mortadella and finish the sandwich, fire up the smoker to 225°F (107°C) and get a good smoke rolling. (For this recipe, wood chips are helpful to get as much smoke as possible in the box.) When the smoker heats up, place the mortadella split-side down on the grate and immediately put the lid on the smoker. Smoke for 30 minutes, just enough to flavor the meat without melting too much of the beautiful interior fat of the charcuterie. Remove and cool completely. When cool, slice as much as you will need for four sandwiches as thinly as possible and set aside. Reserve any extra, well wrapped, in the refrigerator for up to 1 month.

Heat a cast iron skillet over high heat. When hot, add the thinly sliced mortadella in a single layer and let fry in its own fat as it renders. Let the meat get crispy on the edges and add the American cheese. Remove from the heat and set aside.

Gently toast the brioche buns and top with the mortadella and cheese slices. Spoon a heavy dollop of the aioli over the meat and cheese and add the top bun. Serve immediately.

Makes 4 sandwiches, with plenty of mortadella and a little aioli left over

AIOLI

2 large egg yolks

4 teaspoons (20 ml) freshly squeezed lemon juice

1 teaspoon Dijon mustard

½ cup (120 ml) extra virgin olive oil

6 tablespoons (90 ml) canola oil

4 garlic cloves, finely minced or run through a garlic press

Kosher salt and freshly ground black pepper

MORTADELLA SANDWICHES

1 loaf (3 pounds, or 1.4 kg) mortadella from the butcher's counter, halved lengthwise

4 slices American cheese

4 brioche buns, split

BUTTER OF THE GODS

Let's talk luxury and sublime brilliance. This butter is decadent excess like taking a private jet to the Maldives. If smoked bone marrow isn't one of the seven deadly sins, then let's make it number eight. Yet, cooking it is so easy to do, and it will impress everyone (including your dog!). This recipe is scaled so that you could share it with a few friends while the meat cooks for the rest of the party. Of course, as a "butter," it can also be the perfect toast topping, go right on top of a sizzling steak, season up some clams . . . you name it. Make sure to have your neighborhood butcher split the femur bones lengthwise to expose the delicious bone marrow!

2 beef femur bones, split lengthwise

2 tablespoons (28 ml) extra virgin olive oil

1 tablespoon (12 g) Meat Mitch Steer Season Rub, store-bought or homemade (see page 31)

1 lemon, halved

1 loaf sourdough bread, sliced

Fire up your smoker to 250°F (120°C) and get a heavy smoke rolling. Keep the temp around 250°F (120°C) because you don't want to melt the marrow too quickly.

Rinse the bones with cold water before seasoning to make sure there is no debris from the bandsaw that was used to cut them apart. Pat dry with paper towels. Drizzle the cut sides of the bones with the olive oil and then dust with the Meat Mitch Steer Season Rub.

Lay the bones cut-side up on the smoker grate and immediately close the lid. Smoke the bones for approximately 45 minutes until the temperature of the marrow reaches 150°F (66°C) with an instant-read thermometer. While the marrow cooks, toast the bread.

Gently remove the bones from the smoker and place on a serving plate. Squeeze the lemon juice all over the bones and serve immediately with toasted sourdough bread. Provide a small spoon to get all the deliciousness out of the bone.

Serves about 4

SMOKED LAMB CHOPS WITH ASIAN BUTTER SAUCE

Wham, bam, let's hammer some lamb! I have made this for several years in a row for our neighborhood block party. When you bring ribs or brisket, everyone digs right in. Lamb will get you some strange looks at first, but after just one bite they come around. It's charred and smoky on the outside and buttery on the inside. Now all the neighbors ask me where they are if I don't bring them! The sauce is off the chain, marrying Asian flavor with barbecue for something different than your average sauce. These are a showstopper!

To prepare the smoked lamb, set the smoker to 225°F (107°C) and get a good smoke rolling.

In a small bowl, mix the salt and pepper. Coat the lamb with the salt and pepper mixture.

Place the lamb chops in the smoker, insert a digital probe meat thermometer, and cook until the internal temp reaches 125°F (52°C), about an hour. Remove from the smoker and set aside.

Lower your grates directly over the fire or alternatively, crank up a charcoal or gas grill to get it as hot as you can. Grill the lamb chops on all sides until nice and charred, about 1 minute on each side. Remove and let rest while you make the sauce.

To make the Asian Butter Sauce, combine the chicken stock, oyster sauce, lime juice, sugar, and five-spice powder in a saucepan and bring to a boil. Reduce the sauce to ¾ cup (175 ml), about 12 minutes. When the sauce is reduced, remove from the heat and stir in the green onions. Whisk in the butter, one piece at a time, until the sauce is thick and luxurious.

Carve the lamb racks into chops. Serve with the Asian Butter Sauce.

Serves 4 as a main dish

SMOKED LAMB

2 tablespoons (30 g) kosher salt

1 tablespoon (6 g) freshly ground black pepper

2 racks of lamb, bones Frenched and cleaned of fat

ASIAN BUTTER SAUCE

1 cup (235 ml) chicken stock

5 tablespoons (90 g) oyster sauce

¼ cup (60 ml) freshly squeezed lime juice (from 2 limes)

1 tablespoon (13 g) sugar

1 teaspoon Chinese five-spice powder

2 green onions, white and green parts, thinly sliced

½ cup (1 stick, or 112 g) unsalted butter, cut into pieces and chilled

THE JACKKNIFE

My partner, Mark Kelpe, nicknamed Char Bar as the "House of Meat" Char Bar because the menu showcases a ton of smoked meat, while playfully identifying all vegetarian menu items with a skull and crossbones disclaimer reading, "*WARNING: THESE ITEMS CONTAIN NO MEAT!!*" He even drafted our mission statement to read, "We've created a new kind of barbecue playground where both carnivores and herbivores can mingle peacefully. Together, we will be called Charbarians." So, it was our first order of business to make the best meatless smoked jackfruit sandwich that we had ever tasted. Thus, The Jackknife was born. This sandwich continues to win the award for the Best Vegetarian Sandwich in Kansas City year after year.

2 cans (14 ounces, or 390 g each) organic young green jackfruit in water (not brine or syrup)

½ cup (132 g) Char Bar Table Sauce, store-bought or homemade (see page 29)

4 potato buns (I prefer Martin's), sliced open

¼ cup (½ stick, or 56 g) unsalted butter, melted

4 slices provolone cheese

1 ripe avocado, peeled and seeded

24 Crispy Jalapeño Strips (see page 78)

Set your smoker (see Tip below) to 175 to 220°F (79.5 to 104.5°C) and get a good smoke rolling. I prefer apple wood for this smoke.

Drain the jackfruit and lightly pound the flesh with your fist so it spreads out and resembles pieces of pulled pork. Spread out the jackfruit on your smoker's wire racks and smoke for 25 to 30 minutes until the flesh begins to darken. Remove from the smoker and toss with the Char Bar Table Sauce until evenly combined. At this point, the jackfruit can be refrigerated for up to 5 days. Just reheat gently in a shallow saucepan over low heat when you are ready to assemble your sandwiches.

Preheat the broiler. Brush the insides of the potato buns with melted butter and place cut-side up on a baking sheet.

Divide the sauced jackfruit into four equal piles on the baking sheet next to buttered buns and top each pile of jackfruit with 1 slice of provolone cheese. Place on the middle rack of the oven and broil for 30 to 60 seconds until the buns are toasted and the cheese is melted.

Slice the avocado into 16 slices; fan 4 avocado slices on top of each melted cheese. Using a metal spatula, transfer each warm jackfruit pile to the bottom half of a toasted bun. Top each with 6 Crispy Jalapeño Strips and cover with top bun.

TIP: At Char Bar, we use a separate cold smoker for the vegetarian jackfruit, so there is no cross-contamination with meats, but if you don't have a cold smoker, a regular hot smoker works just as well.

Serves 4 with sandwiches that taste so good, you'll swear you're eating pulled pork

SMOKED JALAPEÑO-CHEDDAR BOUDIN

I love New Orleans, and every so often I get an intense craving not only for that city, but for that city's boudin. The flavors and texture of that sausage are unlike anything else. It's such a soft and sumptuous sausage, and the Cajun spices take it to another level. I am shocked that it appears to be enjoyed in a relatively small geographic area and is not celebrated and scarfed down throughout the world like the superhero meat it truly is. I can't encourage you enough to take on this fun weekend project. You won't regret it . . . and cleaning the garage can wait anyway!

In a large pot, combine the pork, chicken livers, onion, bell pepper, celery, garlic, bay leaves, and thyme. Cover with water and add 2 tablespoons (30 g) of the kosher salt and 2 teaspoons of the pepper. Bring this bad boy to a boil and then turn down to a simmer. Grab a slotted spoon and skim off any grey gunk that floats to the top. Keep cooking for an hour or so. You'll want the pork butt to be tender, so make sure to pull a little out and check to see if it's done. While it's stewing, get your meat grinder and sausage stuffer ready for action.

When the pork butt is ready to rock, remove the bay leaves and thyme and discard. Strain everything from the broth and set aside on a tray. Make sure you save that broth. We are going to need it later.

Grind the pork and chicken livers through the small die into a large bowl while it's all still a little hot. (If you don't have a grinder, run through a food mill or pulse in a food processor until minced and transfer to a large bowl.)

Fold in the cooked rice with the green onions, parsley, jalapeños, and the remaining 2 tablespoons (30 g) of Kosher salt and 2 teaspoons of pepper. Stir in some of that cooking liquid you saved, maybe 1 cup (235 ml) or so, to make sure that the forcemeat is a little wet. The rice is going to drink it up, so don't be shy.

Cool the mix completely and then fold in the Velveeta. Stuff the sausages into the casings and set in the fridge, uncovered, for at least 4 hours, but they are best left to rest overnight.

Set your smoker to our sweet spot, around 225°F (107°C), and get a good smoke rolling. Smoke the boudin with a digital probe meat thermometer in place for 1½ to 2 hours until they reach an internal temperature of 145°F (63°C) and get nice and smoky. Serve immediately with ice cold beer and some grainy mustard.

TIPS: This is an intense recipe, and you'll need the right equipment to stuff your casings. I have a food grinder attachment that fits on the end of my KitchenAid mixer and I love to use a hand-cranked sausage stuffer. If you don't have a grinder attachment, you can grind the meat in a food mill or food processor. You can order casings online or you can call your local butcher to see if they have them. Soak the casings to get rid of the salt that preserves them, making sure to change the water a few times. And if you want to skip the whole step of stuffing, just ball up the sausage and smoke or pan-fry. Boudin balls are money, too!

Makes about 2 pounds (900 g) of Louisiana's finest boudin

3 pounds (1.4 kg) pork butt, cubed

½ pound (225 g) fresh chicken livers, rinsed (you can find them in the grocery store)

1 yellow onion, chopped

1 green bell pepper, chopped

2 ribs celery, diced

3 cloves garlic, chopped

2 bay leaves

1 bunch fresh thyme, tied together

4 tablespoons (60 g) kosher salt

4 teaspoons (8 g) freshly ground black pepper

1½ teaspoons ground cayenne, or to taste

6 cups (948 g) cooked and cooled white long-grain rice

1 cup (100 g) thinly sliced green onions, white and green parts

1 cup (60 g) finely chopped flat-leaf parsley

3 jalapeños, stemmed, seeded, and minced

½ pound (225 g) Velveeta, cut into small cubes

5 hog casings, rinsed out very well (see Tips below)

SMOKING SEAFOOD

I grew up in Eastern Pennsylvania, where seafood was king and plentiful thanks to the Maryland coast just an hour and a half away. As a kid, my parents would take me to Inner Harbor on the water, which was my favorite place on Earth. I could not have been happier. Harbor Market, similar to Reading Terminal Market in Philadelphia, is a neighborhood of Who's Who of Eats. I would watch a team of break dancers out front and then enter a food emporium of culinary riches. One stand stood next to another, and seafood was everywhere. Phillips Seafood was a mainstay that we would hit for blue crabs. When I think about those crabs loaded with Old Bay Seasoning today, I want them to be my last supper (though I would add plenty of cold beer).

Smoking fish and shellfish is different than working with big hunks of meat. Check in with your light and delicate side, Pods. You'll need to be a little more precise with your approach and keep an eye on these lean meats from the sea. Pork, beef, and chicken can be forgiving if you take them a touch too far on the smoker; they might not end up being perfect, but they'll be okay. But fish and shellfish quickly can go from sweet and tender to dry and chalky if you don't pay attention.

The most common things I smoke when hanging out with friends or on the night before a competition are old standbys: lobsters, salmon, shrimp, clams, mussels, and oysters. You can't go wrong with them, but if you want to go further, I have more unique recipes, like my Bourbon Sweet Tea Smoked Salmon and Smoked Clams Casino, which are both great for entertaining. No matter whether you try one of my recipes or go your own way, you'll need some techniques to get the seafood ready.

THE ALL-IMPORTANT BRINE

You've probably worked with brines before, likely around Thanksgiving, where you give a big bird a bath in salty water to pump it full of extra moisture and flavor. This same logic is needed for fish and shellfish, though I make a brine that has a little bit less salt and sugar than brines for other meats. Here's a basic recipe that you can make your own depending on the seafood. You can use it as is, but I often like to add fresh herbs, different kinds of peppercorns, and citrus zest depending on what I'm going for. Have fun replacing the sugar (try brown sugar!) and flavored salts as well. Brine the fish and shellfish for 12 hours, then drain, discard the brine, and pat the food dry. Smoke or grill to perfection and enjoy!

BASIC SEAFOOD BRINE

1 quart (946 ml) water

2 tablespoons (30 g) kosher salt

1½ tablespoons (20 g) granulated sugar

Mix all the ingredients in a bowl and whisk until the salt and sugar are completely dissolved. Get this really cold in the fridge before adding any seafood.

Makes about 1 quart (946 ml) (enough for 3 pounds [1.4 kg] of seafood)

HOT AND FAST SMOKING FOR CLAMS, MUSSELS, AND OYSTERS

For smoking clams, mussels, and oysters, you need to go the opposite way of what we do for pork and beef. We want to cook these guys pretty hot so that they will open up, while not giving them time to dry out. I like to either stoke the fire and set them right in the firebox or dial up the temp on the smoker to about 350°F (180°C) for these guys.

We also want to pummel these guys with smoke since they won't cook for long. I like to use little wood chips for shellfish, since they create a lot of smoke quickly. Get a lot of smoke rolling and then place the brined clams, mussels, or shucked oysters directly on the grill grate and close the lid to retain heat. When the clam and mussel shells pop open and the meat is juicy and plump, they're done. Oysters are done when they are opaque and just barely cooked through. Don't dry 'em out, Jimmy. It would be better to undercook these guys than turn them into rubber bullets.

Remove the shellfish from the grill and serve immediately. Toss any clams and mussels that don't open and don't try to force any open. If it's meant to be, it's meant to be, Pods!

LOBSTER AND SHRIMP

The keys for tender shrimp and lobsters are to brine them and to keep them in the shell for smoking. The shells act like a barrier that magically brings smoke in while not letting too much juiciness out.

I like to smoke shrimp and lobster (shells on!) at higher temps than land meats, but lower than oysters, clams, and mussels. The thinking is that the shrimp and lobsters are a little bit thicker and more resilient. I'll usually shoot for 275°F (140°C).

Timing and temperature are going to be key as well. You want to cook most large shrimp and lobsters for 25 to 30 minutes and only take them to an internal temperature of about 130°F (54.5°C).

Serve with lots of lemon wedges for squeezing over.

A NOTE ON PREPARING OYSTERS FOR THE SMOKER

Shucking oysters is not difficult to learn, but it takes a little patience and practice to get really good at it. The key is to hold the oyster in a towel or wear a glove so you don't impale yourself. That's an ouch! You can also place the oyster on a cutting board to keep it from sliding all over the place. Hold the oyster, making sure you've got the curved side facing down and the flatter side facing up when you are shucking. Using your oyster knife, wiggle the tip of the knife in the pointed end of the oyster. You'll likely see a little nook and that's your spot! Jiggle the knife gently and then twist the knife to pop the oyster open, making sure not to lose any of the juice or "liquor" inside. Slide the knife fully to detach the muscle from the top shell and then lift that shell off. Now, the oysters are ready for the smoker; brining isn't necessary.

GRILLED CORN & DUNGENESS CRAB DIP WITH JALAPEÑOS

For the last several years in mid-September, I have traveled to see my longtime friend John Pontz in Seattle, Washington. He picks me up at the airport and we run to Pike Place Market so we can watch them chuck the fish around and ogle the unbelievable array of some of the world's best seafood. I generally buy huge shrimp, scallops, and, always, halibut cheeks. Then, we head north to Anacortes where we drive onto a ferry and head to his house on Shaw Island. It's an amazing place where deer freely graze all over the waterfront property. We unpack and then prepare to catch the star of the show, Dungeness crabs. Every morning, we head out into the water and check our traps. I have never been disappointed with our daily harvest—crazy amounts of gigantic Dungeness crabs, sometime twelve male keepers in one trap (but we could only keep five)! With so much crab throughout the week, we are constantly making and trying new recipes and ideas. This appetizer dip is a showstopper every time, with grilled corn, melty hot cheese, spicy jalapeños and chiles, and the star—jumbo lumps of succulent crab.

Fire up a charcoal or gas grill and get it nice and hot. Go ahead and turn your oven on to 350°F (180°C, or gas mark 4) as well.

Toss the ears of corn with olive oil and season with salt and pepper. Throw the ears on the grill, turning them until you achieve a nice char on the kernels all the way around, about 3 to 4 minutes. Then, use a knife to cut off the kernels.

Combine the cheese, green chiles, jalapeños, cilantro, cumin, mayonnaise, sour cream, chili garlic sauce, and hot sauce in a large bowl and mix well.

Stir in the corn and salt. Gently fold in the crabmeat, keeping the lumps whole. Pour it all into a badass Dutch oven or any good dish and bake for 30 to 40 minutes until the mix is bubbly and golden brown. Serve with tortilla scoops, yep.

TIP: Lump Dungeness is the way to go but, if you must, you can substitute any lump crabmeat here. It's all golden, Podsy.

Makes 1½ quarts (1.4 L) of delicious cheesy dip

3 ears of corn, husked

¼ cup (60 ml) extra virgin olive oil

Salt and toasted black peppercorns (see page 181)

2 cups (225 g) shredded sharp cheddar cheese

½ can (4 ounces, or 115 g) chopped green chiles

2 tablespoons (11 g) chopped fresh jalapeños

2 tablespoons (2 g) chopped fresh cilantro

1½ teaspoons ground cumin

½ cup (115 g) mayonnaise (I prefer Duke's)

1 cup (230 g) sour cream

1 teaspoon chili garlic sauce

1 teaspoon hot sauce (I prefer Valentina Mexican hot sauce)

1 pound (455 g) smoked lump Dungeness crab (see page 130 for info on smoking) (see Tip below)

Tortilla scoops, to serve

BOURBON SWEET TEA SMOKED SALMON

Most people I know have a love-hate relationship with salmon. Here's one way to make everyone fall in love: add smoke, bourbon, and sweet tea. This recipe has incredible flavor and the bourbon blends well with the sweetness of the tea and brown sugar. You'll need to cure the salmon the night before, but the process is totally worth it. I like to start smoking as the fire is burning down from a different smoke and there aren't many coals left.

½ cup (100 g) granulated sugar

½ cup (115 g) packed light brown sugar

1 tablespoon (6 g) freshly ground black pepper

½ cup (120 g) kosher salt

½ cup (120 ml) bourbon

1 cup (235 ml) brewed sweet tea, cold

1½- to 2-pound (680 to 900 g) salmon fillet, skin on, pin bones removed

1 lemon, sliced into rounds

To make the brine, mix the granulated sugar, brown sugar, black pepper, and salt in a medium mixing bowl. Add the bourbon and sweet tea and whisk until the sugars and salt dissolve. The mix will be a little syrupy.

Put the salmon in a large 1-gallon (3.8 L) zip top storage bag. Pour the brine into the bag. Place the lemon slices in last and close the bag. Let sit overnight, flipping from top to bottom two or three times during the cure.

The next day, remove the salmon from the bag and discard the brine and lemon slices. Rinse the salmon under cool water and pat dry with paper towels. Refrigerate until you are ready to smoke it or for up to 2 days.

Set your smoker at 200°F (93°C), or when the smoker cools down to 200°F (93°C), go get the salmon, pat dry again, and then place it on the grates of the smoker. Put the lid on and then add some small wood chips to the firebox, adding more chips as needed to get a lot of smoke on the fish quickly. Cook for 2 hours or until the fish reaches an internal temperature of 145°F (63°C) on a digital probe meat thermometer.

Remove the fish from the smoker and place skin-side up on a cutting board. Gently peel the skin off and discard. Carefully flip the fish back over, cut the fillet into four pieces, and serve immediately.

TIP: This is also really good when you cool the fish and just flake the meat straight off of the skin. It's really great the next day with bagels and cream cheese.

Serves 4 as an excellent main course

NEW YEAR'S SMOKED CLAMS CASINO

I remember hearing the name Clams Casino as a kid and thinking I wanted to grow up and be rich so I could eat them every day. With this recipe, let's kick it up with some champagne and celebrate now that we are all so rich and sophisticated! Bacon, butter, garlic, and onions go on the clams. We could stop there, but I like to bring on the fruit and nuttiness of Parmigiano-Reggiano cheese, along with a hint of smoke. If I were a clam, I would open up for that 8 days a week.

Set your smoker at 325°F (170°C) and get a good smoke rolling. This will take a little extra charcoal, but it's worth it. When the smoker is ready, place a large, high-sided, cast iron skillet right in the coals of your fire box. Immediately add the bacon and cook until the fat has rendered and the bacon is lightly browned and crisp, about 5 minutes. If it gets too hot, bring the skillet up to the top grate to allow it to cook with less intensity.

Stir in the onions and garlic and cook, stirring often, until onions have softened, 3 to 4 minutes.

Add the clams and "bubbly" and give the pan a quick shake. Cover the skillet with a piece of aluminum foil and cook until the clams open up, which should take only 2 or 3 minutes. Check under the foil and continue to cook until all the clams have opened—if there's a stubborn bugger in there that won't open, throw it away. Remove the foil and then bring the pan to your worktable, making sure to have a trivet or hot pad under to protect the work surface.

Using a slotted spoon, transfer the shellfish to a large bowl to cool off enough to handle. Place the skillet back on the grate and reduce the liquid until about ¼ cup (60 ml) is left. You can tell when it gets a little thick and bubbly. Pour the liquid into a small mixing bowl and stir in the butter and all of the herbs. When cool, add in the Parmigiano-Reggiano cheese and season with the Meat Mitch Competition WHOMP! Rub and set aside.

Using an oyster or butter knife (nothing sharp here), gently remove the top half of each clam shell and throw in the garbage. Loosen each piece of clam meat from the bottom halves of the shells and then gently place back in the shells.

Scoop about 1 teaspoon of your bacon butter into each clam. If there is any left, try to split it evenly among the clams. Top with the panko breadcrumbs. Place each clam back into the skillet as tight as you can, making sure they all fit in one layer.

Throw some woodchips into the smoker to blast it with quick, fresh smoke, close the smoker door or lid, and bake these bad boys, uncovered, in the smoker for 20 minutes or until the tops are toasted and brown. Carefully remove the skillet and place on a hot pad. Squeeze the lemon halves all over and serve immediately.

Serves 6 as a pregame appetizer

¼ pound (115 g) bacon, minced

¾ cup (120 g) minced yellow onion

4 cloves garlic, minced

2 dozen Littleneck or Cherrystone clams, thoroughly rinsed and scrubbed

⅓ cup (82 ml) Prosecco or Champagne

1 cup (2 sticks, or 225 g) unsalted butter, at room temperature

2 tablespoons (8 g) chopped fresh flat-leaf parsley

1 tablespoon (4 g) chopped fresh tarragon leaves

1 tablespoon (3 g) chopped fresh basil leaves

⅓ cup (80 g) packed freshly grated Parmigiano-Reggiano cheese

1 teaspoon Meat Mitch Competition WHOMP! Rub, store-bought or homemade (see page 28)

1 cup (112 g) panko breadcrumbs

1 lemon, cut in half

BEST CRAB CAKES EVER

I am passionate about crab cakes and rarely, if ever, order them out as I'm almost always disappointed. They're too often filled with some gooey, doughy filler. (I'm not into eating anything referred to as "binder.") I can smell it on the plate before it gets to me, and I know it's bad. Herein lies the problem: I love crab cakes and I want to eat only the best ever made.

During a spring break trip with our kids a few years back, I found what I believed to be a perfect crab cake at Bud & Alley's in Seaside, Florida. They had a golden crust covered in a lemon sauce. They smelled amazing—amazingly like crabmeat. The cakes were packed with lump crabmeat and there appeared to be no filler at all—just great, buttery, lump crab flavor and heaps of it! I begged the waiter to tell me how they did it, but he didn't know. I went back three more times and asked every time. Eventually, I gathered the basics: they mixed the crab with heavy whipping cream and froze the patties to keep them together—eliminating the need for the doughy filler/binder in the first place. Genius! So, I went to work. After several attempts, I refined the seasoning and landed on a recipe that will kick up your taste buds and bring out the great flavor of the packed lump crabmeat. Here is exactly how to make the best crab cakes *ever*!

½ cup (1 stick, or 112 g) unsalted butter, plus 1 tablespoon (14 g)

2 celery ribs, minced

½ yellow onion, minced

½ teaspoon freshly ground black pepper, preferably toasted (see page 181), plus more as needed

1 teaspoon (2 g) plus 1 tablespoon (7 g) Old Bay Seasoning

1 tablespoon (15 ml) hot sauce (I prefer Valentina Mexican hot sauce)

2 pounds (900 g) smoked jumbo lump crabmeat (see page 130 for info on smoking seafood)

6 tablespoons (90 ml) heavy whipping cream

3 large eggs

26 Ritz crackers, crushed

Vegetable oil, for pan-frying

Lemon Beurre Blanc Sauce (recipe follows)

2 tablespoons (8 g) chopped fresh flat-leaf parsley

2 lemons, cut into wedges for garnish

Let's make some clarified butter first. Heat 1 stick of butter in a small pot over low heat until the solids separate. Skim off the white foam that rises to the top with a little ladle and pour the clear butter aside to cool.

In another small pot, melt the remaining 1 tablespoon (14 g) of butter and add the minced celery and onion as well as the ½ teaspoon of black pepper and the 1 teaspoon of Old Bay Seasoning. Cover and sweat this over medium-low heat for about 10 minutes or until the vegetables are nice and soft. It's going to smell amazing, but don't start eating now!

Remove the veggies from the heat and let them cool down. Transfer the veggies plus the clarified butter and the Valentina hot sauce to a large mixing bowl. Add the crab and heavy whipping cream and mix gently. I repeat, gently! The worst thing you could do here is overmix the crab and break up the fat lumps we just paid a premium for!

Cover and place this mixture in the freezer for 30 minutes or so. Remove and form the mix into 5-ounce (140 g) balls (the size of a snowball) in your hands. Again, be gentle; you aren't packing these snowballs for war. You should be able to get six good ones out of the mix. Cover in plastic wrap and then return to the freezer for at least 4 hours or up to overnight. You gotta get these nice and cold since we aren't using that filler/binder nonsense in these crab cakes.

While the mix is chilling, whip your eggs in a small mixing bowl with a crack of freshly ground black pepper. Add the crushed Ritz crackers to another bowl with the remaining 1 tablespoon (7 g) of Old Bay Seasoning. Go ahead and preheat the oven to 350°F (180°C, or gas mark 4) for later.

recipe continues

Remove the frozen crab cakes from the freezer and dunk them in the egg and then into the seasoned Ritz crumble mix. Cover completely. Repeat with all of the crab cakes and set aside. Get about ⅛ inch (3 mm) of your vegetable oil ripping hot in a cast iron pan over coals on the grill. I like to cook these crab cakes outside in order to keep the oil smell from taking over the kitchen. There's nothing better than a cast iron skillet over hot coals. Okay, if you must, place over your gas stove at home. Get it hot. I like to drip water droplets in to see when the oil is hot enough. The droplets will sizzle and pop, and that's how you know it's ready.

Carefully drop the crab cakes in the pan and press down on them lightly just to slightly flatten them so they appear a little more cake-like and lay nicely on your plate. Fry for 4 to 5 minutes on each side until you have made a perfect golden crust (don't burn the outside). Then, put the entire cast iron skillet in the oven for 20 minutes. If desired, you can use a fish spatula or a slotted spoon to transfer the cakes to a baking sheet—and leave the oil smell outside.

After 20 minutes, remove from the oven and plate up! You can serve the Lemon Beurre Blanc on the side, but I like to ladle it directly on top of the cake and sprinkle some parsley all over. Drop a few lemon wedges on the plate and devour.

Makes 6 of the best crab cakes ever

LEMON BEURRE BLANC

¼ cup (40 g) chopped yellow onion

1 cup (235 ml) dry white wine, like a Sauvignon Blanc or Pinot Grigio

1 sprig of fresh thyme

Finely grated zest of 1 lemon

¼ cup (60 ml) freshly squeezed lemon juice

1 tablespoon (15 ml) heavy whipping cream

¾ cup (1½ sticks, or 167 g) unsalted butter, sliced and chilled

½ teaspoon kosher salt

¼ teaspoon ground white pepper

This sauce is the perfect soulmate for crab cakes, fish, vegetables, potatoes, your mother-in-law—you name it! A lemony burst of magic wakes up the palate and brings everything it touches to life.

Combine the onion, wine, thyme, lemon zest, and lemon juice in a saucepan and bring to a boil over medium-high heat. Cook it down until it is almost dry, about 5 minutes. Remove the thyme sprig.

Add the cream and heat until it bubbles up. Remove from the heat and let cool for just about 30 seconds. Remove the diced butter from the fridge and whisk in one or two slices at a time. Whisk fast; we are making a fancy emulsion here. Continue to add the butter slices and season with salt and white pepper. The sauce should be rich and velvety. Set aside in a warm, but not hot place—or even in a little Thermos—until you are ready to serve.

Your sauce will break if it gets too hot or too cold. If this happens, just warm up a little more heavy whipping cream and then slowly whisk in the broken sauce. It should come back together!

Makes about 1 cup (235 ml)

CRAIG VERHAGE
THE BBQ NINJA
YAZOO CITY, MISSISSIPPI

Man, do I love this guy. The best thing about backyard barbecue and competition barbecue is the community and friendships you build—hands down. I met Craig Verhage over a decade ago at our first Memphis in May World Championship Barbecue Cooking Contest. Due to flooding, the event was forced to move from Tom Lee Park on the Mississippi River to the Liberty Bowl Memorial Stadium. We weren't happy about the venue change, but we were excited to be there regardless. Fortunately, we were positioned down the row from an iconic Memphis in May BBQ team, the Ubons out of Yazoo City, Mississippi.

Just say the word Yazoo . . . it's hysterical, fun, exciting, energetic, and eye-opening, all the things that sum up the Ubons BBQ team from the great Poppy Roark, the patriarch, to Leslie Roark Scott, the barbecue princess, and my pal, Craig Verhage, the BBQ Ninja! There are too many to name from this team, but each member is special and took us in as family from day one.

One of my favorite memories happened after Meat Mitch won Grand Champion in the Beef Category at the Memphis in May World Championship Barbecue Cooking Contest: I was on Cloud Nine. We went in search of my boy Craig and the Ubons team to celebrate together. Storms were rolling in and the skies were dark when we reached their tent. I saw my longtime friend Alan Campbell of the Ubons team, and he congratulated us and high fives and hugs ensued. I asked, "Where is Craig?!" He said (in a deep Mississippi accent), "You see that sky up there? He gone! When it comes to lightning, he been struck twice!" We all laughed so hard, but when it comes to all-around great guys and fantastic pitmasters, Craig Verhage is here to stay!

Photo by Heath Scott, courtesy of Craig Verhage

ROYAL OAK'S SMOKED ALLIGATOR ROLLS

RECIPE BY CRAIG VERHAGE

Do you wanna smoke a reptile that can grow up to 19 feet (5.8 m) in length and swallow your head? I do! My buddy Craig Verhage aka The BBQ Ninja is famous for this Bayou classic. He wrestles these things when people are not looking. Chicken? The Ninja isn't chicken, but the gator doesn't taste far from it. The meat is white and quite tender and packed with flavor. Craig's recipes bring these flavors to the forefront and what a spectacle it will be at your next neighborhood function. Whole hog? Nope. We goin' whole gator!

ALLIGATOR

1 cup (225 g) packed light brown sugar

1 cup (240 g) kosher salt

1 gallon (3.8 L) apple cider vinegar

10 pounds (4.6 kg) ice

1 whole alligator, dressed (see Tip below)

1 cup (192 g) Meat Mitch Competition WHOMP! Rub, store-bought or homemade (see page 28)

1½ cups (420 g) Meat Mitch Competition WHOMP! BBQ Sauce, store-bought or homemade (see page 32)

STUFFED ROLLS

4 pounds (1.8 kg) Smoked Jalapeño-Cheddar Boudin (see page 129) or other boudin

1½ pounds (680 g) cream cheese

2 packs (4.3 ounces, or 120.5 g each) Hormel Original Real Crumbled Bacon Bits

3 packets (1 ounce, or 28 g each) Hidden Valley Ranch Spicy Ranch Dressing

40–50 hot dog buns

To make the smoked alligator, mix together the brown sugar, salt, vinegar, and ice in a cooler. Add the alligator and then add water until the gator is covered. Let the gator brine overnight and then remove, pat dry, and dust with the Meat Mitch Competition WHOMP! Rub.

Set your smoker to 250°F (120°C) and get a good smoke rolling. I really like to smoke with apple or peach wood, so the smoke flavor is not overpowering and also won't compromise the color.

Insert your trusty probe thermometer, put the gator on the grate, and get your first beer. When the thickest part of the tail reaches 160°F (71°C), glaze the whole gator with the Meat Mitch Competition WHOMP! BBQ Sauce and keep smoking until the thickest part of the tail reaches 170°F (77°C). This should take 4 to 5 hours, so plan ahead!

Meanwhile, start working on the stuffing for the roll. Mix together the boudin, cream cheese, bacon bits, and dressing mix with your hands. Form into a loaf. Put in the smoker at 250°F (120°C) and smoke for 4 hours. (Alternatively, you can mix up this stuffing and then stuff it into the gator's tail before you smoke it.)

To serve, remove the gator meat from the top and bottom of the tail. Discard any clear fat you see on the meat. This is very important because it will have a fishy taste that you won't love! Chop up the meat.

Put some stuffing on a hot dog bun and then sprinkle the chopped alligator meat onto it and add some barbecue sauce over the top. (This stuffing is good inside anything.) Cut in half and serve.

TIP: Whole gators average about 30 pounds (13.6 kg) and you can buy them at lacrawfish.com. The Louisiana Crawfish Company is an amazing resource for all things Cajun. They'll even send live crawfish to you via FedEx!

Makes about 40 to 50 servings

Photo by Heath Scott, courtesy of Craig Verhage

4

WHAT TO DO WITH YOUR 'QUE

Briskets weighing 16 pounds (7.3 kg), pork butts the size of basketballs . . . how are we going to eat all of this?! Leftovers, for me, used to mean reheating that meat or peeling the foil off the mashed potatoes the next day. Not anymore! I've discovered there are many ways to turn your prized proteins into dining room delicacies.

In this chapter, we'll travel to the east coast and make an amazing riff on Philly cheesesteaks and an elevated take on scrapple. We'll stuff biscuits with briskets and pile pork into steamed buns. By the end, you won't be afraid to get cheeky with tacos and you may even find a way to dance the merengue thanks to a Barbe-Cuban sandwich.

Whip open the fridge and grab those leftovers because you, my friend, have some work to do!

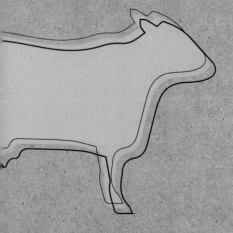

PIG MAC

I love New Orleans. Love it. It's gritty, beautiful, artistic, musical, festive, and most of all *delicious*! I have been to NOLA for bachelor parties, business junkets, barbecue competitions . . . and sometimes I just sneak off for a weekend and don't tell anyone. Cochon is my favorite restaurant in the city. When I met the chef/co-owner, Stephen Stryjewski, at Hogs for the Cause BBQ Competition, he encouraged me to hit up his other location, Cochon Butcher, for lunch. I stopped by and ordered his Le Pig Mac sando along with boudin. Both were stunning.

This is my riff on his iconic sandwich. You'll start with leftover pulled pork shoulder and pulled rib meat and mix it with fresh ground beef from the market to make an incredible-tasting patty. Of course, there's a Secret Sauce! Our version is addictive and has just a touch of smoke. (It's great as a remoulade for seafood as well.)

1 cup (236 g) cold pulled pork (see Competition-Style Pulled Pork, page 51), chopped

¼ cup (59 g) leftover pulled rib meat (see Competition-Style St. Louis Spare Ribs, page 46), chopped

1½ pounds (680 g) ground beef, preferably 80 percent lean

1 tablespoon (12 g) Meat Mitch's Competition WHOMP! Rub, store-bought or homemade (see page 28)

2 tablespoons (28 ml) canola oil

1 cup (43 g) shredded iceberg lettuce

8 slices American cheese

4 teaspoons (13 g) chopped white onion

4 hamburger buns (Make sure they have sesame seeds!)

SECRET SAUCE

½ teaspoon kosher salt

2 cloves garlic, minced

½ cup (132 g) Char Bar Table Sauce, store-bought or homemade (see page 29)

¼ cup (60 g) ketchup

1½ cups (340 g) mayonnaise (I prefer Duke's)

½ teaspoon freshly ground black pepper

1 cup (143 g) minced dill pickles

1 cup (160 g) minced white onion

To make the patties, in a large mixing bowl, combine the chopped pork shoulder and rib meat with the ground beef and Meat Mitch Competition WHOMP! Rub. Mix with your hands to combine. Divide the mixture into eight portions and form into burgers. Refrigerate, covered, until you are ready to cook.

To make the sauce, put the salt and garlic on a cutting board. Using a 9-inch (23 cm) chef's knife, mash and massage the ingredients until a paste forms. Scrape the paste into a medium mixing bowl. Add the Char Bar sauce, ketchup, mayonnaise, and black pepper. Mix with a wire whisk until thoroughly blended. Gently fold in the pickles and white onion. Refrigerate, covered, until you are ready to serve.

When you're ready to cook the burgers, heat a cast iron or electric griddle over medium-high heat. Add the canola oil. When the oil just begins to shimmer, add the burgers, pressing down lightly on the meat with the back of a metal spatula. Cook for 2 minutes and flip, lightly pressing on the second side. Cook for 2 minutes and then add a slice of cheese to each patty. Cook for 30 more seconds or until the cheese just begins to soften. Using the metal spatula, transfer the patties to a plate.

While the patties rest for a minute, spread the sauce on both sides of each bun. Place one patty on the bottom of each bun and then top with another patty. Top each burger with pickles and chopped onions and more sauce, if desired. Place the top of the buns on the burgers and serve immediately.

Serves 4

RICH MAN'S SCRAPPLE

Rich man's . . . .what? While I'm a KC royal now, I'm originally from PA. I remember my Dad frying up this block of mush called scrapple, which if you've never had it is like the mid-Atlantic Amish version of Spam. It is usually made up of the less-appreciated parts of the hog that people wouldn't necessary line up for at the counter: pork heart, liver, and even kidney. My friends and I commonly referred to it as "lips and a**." Although I love traditional scrapple, especially Habbersett brand (please try it if you get the chance!), I decided to make a version of this from the best-quality meats (leftover barbecue) and see what happened. While it has the same consistency of classic scrapple, it's deliciously smoky and noticeably richer—hence the name of the dish. It's a great brunch item and is amazing with runny eggs and hot sauce. Please, please, please try this even if the photo doesn't sell you. Taste-wise, I would have made this the cover of the book, but they told me we are trying to sell books, so . . .

3 cups (450 g) chopped leftover smoked meat, preferably a mix of beef, pork, and/or sausage

3 cups (700 ml) chicken or beef broth

½ teaspoon kosher salt

½ teaspoon freshly ground black pepper

¼ teaspoon rubbed sage

¼ teaspoon dried thyme

Pinch of ground cayenne

Pinch of ground cloves

1 cup (140 g) finely ground cornmeal

About 1 cup (125 g) all-purpose flour, to dredge (if you like, seasoned with salt and pepper)

Canola or vegetable oil

Line a loaf pan or lidded plastic container with plastic wrap.

Combine the smoked meats and 1 cup (235 ml) of the broth in a food processor and purée until smooth.

Transfer the purée to a saucepan and add the remaining 2 cups (475 ml) of broth, salt, black pepper, sage, thyme, cayenne, and clove. Bring to a boil and then reduce the heat to a simmer.

Sift in the cornmeal and continuously whisk until the mixture gets very thick (almost too difficult to stir). Remove from the heat and transfer into the prepared loaf pan. Press out any air bubbles. Cover and refrigerate at least 3 hours, preferably overnight.

To prepare for serving, remove the meat from the plastic wrap, slice into 12 ¼ inch (6 mm)-thick slabs, and dredge in the flour. Heat ¼ inch (6 mm) of oil in a cast iron skillet over medium-high heat. Add a single layer of slices and pan-fry on each side for 2 to 3 minutes until brown and crisp. Remove with a slotted spoon and drain on a wire rack or paper towels. (If you don't want to cook all at once, wrap tightly in plastic wrap and store in the refrigerator for up to 1 week.) Serve warm.

Serves 6 to 12 for breakfast or lunch, depending how hungry they are

BBQ STUFFED STEAMED BAO BUNS

The meeting of Asian cuisine and barbecue has become more and more popular. In fact, famous Pitmaster and James Beard winner Aaron Franklin worked with Chef Tyson Cole to open Loro—an Asian smokehouse in Austin, Texas. The idea of mixing different smoked meats with Chinese bao buns (steamed buns) is just one delicious way to enjoy your hard work at the pit. The easiest way to concoct the buns would be to purchase them premade. However, when we make this as a family, my wife makes these buns, which are heavily based on David Chang's from the legendary Momofuku franchise. No matter which way you go, the smoked meats melt into these pillowy treasures, and when you combine them with pickled red onions, quick pickles, and a mix of Meat Mitch Competition WHOMP! BBQ Sauce and hoisin, you'll be wondering how you have not had this before!

Stir together the yeast and 1½ cups (355 ml) room-temperature water in the bowl of a stand mixer fitted with a dough hook. Add the flour, sugar, milk powder, salt, baking powder, baking soda, and pork fat. Mix on the lowest speed setting for 10 minutes. The dough should churn into a ball on the hook. Lightly oil a large bowl and put the dough in it, turning it over to coat it with the oil. Cover the bowl with a clean kitchen towel, put it in a warm place, and let the dough rise until it doubles in size, about 1 hour or maybe a touch longer.

Next, roll out the dough to a thickness of ⅛ inch (3 mm). Using a sharp knife, divide the dough in half and then divide each half into five equal pieces. Don't ask me to do the math, but each piece should weigh 5 ounces (140 g). Roll each piece into a log and then cut each log into 5 pieces, making 50 (1 ounce [28 g]) pieces total. Roll each piece into a ball and set them on baking sheets lined with parchment paper. I like to make them large to hold more meat—so, if you like, you can put two dough balls together and double your action! Cover them loosely with plastic wrap and let them rise for 30 to 40 minutes until they are nice and puffy like dinner rolls. While they're rising, cut out 50 (or 25 if you doubled) 4-inch (10 cm) squares of parchment paper. I know, right?

After 30 to 40 minutes, use a rolling pin to roll each ball into a 4 inch (6 mm)-long oval. Brush lightly with vegetable oil, lay a chopstick horizontally across the center of the oval, and fold the oval over onto itself to form a bun. Gently pull out the chopstick, leaving the bun folded, and transfer it to a square of parchment paper. Put it back under the plastic wrap and form the rest of the buns. Let the buns rest for 45 minutes as they will continue to rise—I like them big and fluffy.

We have a bamboo steamer at home which has multiple layers and works really well. We also have a gas stove, so be careful not to catch this type of steamer on fire. Working in batches so you don't crowd the steamer (this is very important), steam the buns on the parchment squares for 10 to 12 minutes, or until the buns are puffy and spring back quickly when you push with your finger.

recipe continues

1 tablespoon (12 g) plus 1 teaspoon (4 g) active dry yeast

4¼ cups (510 g) bread flour

6 tablespoons (78 g) sugar

3 tablespoons (24 g) nonfat dry milk powder

1 tablespoon (15 g) kosher salt

½ rounded teaspoon baking powder

½ teaspoon baking soda

⅓ cup (80 ml) rendered pork fat from your smoked meat

Vegetable oil

2 pounds (900 g) pulled smoked pork butt or smoked rib meat (see Competition-Style Pulled Pork and Competition-Style St. Louis Spare Ribs, pages 51 and 46)

¾ cup (210 g) Meat Mitch Competition WHOMP! BBQ Sauce, store-bought or homemade (see page 32)

¼ cup (63 g) hoisin sauce

2 cups (310 g) Quick Cured Cucumbers (recipe follows)

1 cup (155 g) Pickled Red Onions (recipe follows)

Sriracha sauce (optional)

Now, it's time to feast! Ditch the parchment paper and start to load the buns with all your delicious treasures. (If you have made too many, which I doubt, you can freeze these bad boys for up to 2 months.) Mix the Meat Mitch Competition WHOMP! BBQ Sauce with the hoisin sauce. To assemble the buns, open a warm bun and spread 1 to 2 teaspoons of the sauce mixture on the inside. Stuff full with smoked meats and then stuff in some cukes and pickled onions. Add a squirt of Sriracha if you like. Repeat with the remaining buns and eat.

TIP: Get online and get yourself real deal commercial plastic wrap, either 12-inch (30 cm) or 24-inch (60 cm). It's worth every penny! The same goes for parchment paper. I like to order off of webrestaurant.com or Amazon.

Makes 25 to 50 buns, depending on size

PICKLED RED ONIONS

¾ cup (175 ml) rice vinegar

3 tablespoons (39 g) sugar

¼ teaspoon kosher salt

¼ teaspoon red pepper flakes

1 large red onion, thinly sliced

In a small, nonreactive saucepan, heat the vinegar, sugar, salt, and red pepper flakes until boiling. Add the onion slices, lower the heat, and then continue to cook for about a minute. Let cool to room temperature. Cover and refrigerate until it's time to serve.

TIP: Try using different vinegars with this recipe. I love it with apple cider vinegar, and it's even good with distilled white vinegar.

Makes about 2½ cups (310 g)

QUICK CURED CUCUMBERS

2 thick Kirby or pickling cucumbers, cut into ⅛-inch (3 mm) slices

1 teaspoon kosher salt

1 tablespoon (13 g) granulated sugar

These are so easy to make and taste so good; they can enhance any meal with their added pop of sweetness and crunch.

Combine the cucumbers with the sugar and salt in a small mixing bowl and toss to coat. Let sit for 5 to 10 minutes. Use right away or refrigerate for up to 4 hours.

TIP: Most cucumbers will work for this, but Kirby's have the best crunch and color. Try these on pulled pork sandwiches, too.

Makes about 2 cups (310 g)

POUTINE WITH SMOKED MEAT GRAVY

Poutine is just a fancy word for throwing tasty stuff on French fries. And I can't think of a better way to repurpose the weekend's barbecue than doing just that! There's no need to fire up the deep fryer; the toppings are the star of the show and these fries will disappear in a minute. Mound a plate high with the fries, gravy, and meat, and, oh yeah, let's throw some cheese curds on top, too, *because we can!*

Preheat the oven according to the package directions to get your fries ready to bake off.

While your oven is getting nice and toasty, let's make the star of the show here: the gravy. In a saucepan, melt the bacon fat over medium heat. When hot, add the onions and cook for about 10 minutes or until they are nice and soft. Add the flour and stir with a whisk. Continue to cook until the mix (or "roux" to your inner Frenchman) just turns brown, about 8 minutes. Be careful not to burn it!

Crank it to high heat and immediately add the stock and whisk quickly. The mix will bubble like crazy, but will simmer down after a few seconds. Keep cooking until the gravy comes to a boil and thickens. Add the bounty of smoked meats and stir it up. Season with salt to taste. Skim and discard any foam that collects on the side of the pan. Turn your heat down and let it barely simmer while you bake your fries.

Spread out the fries on a baking sheet and follow the package directions for baking.

As soon as the fries are baked, season them with the Meat Mitch Competition WHOMP! Rub and place in a mixing bowl. Toss with the cheese curds and then place all of this into a serving bowl.

Douse the fries with the gravy and assess the mess. Top with chopped parsley if you'd like to put lipstick on the hog, so to speak.

TIPS: Instead of bacon grease, rendered fat from your pork butts is great, too! Butter works as well. Cheese curds made their way into a lot of grocery store aisles a few years ago and can also be purchased online.

Serves 6 to 8 people as a drunken, late-night salvation

¼ cup (56 g) leftover smoked bacon grease (see Tips below)

½ cup (80 g) finely chopped yellow onion

¼ cup (31 g) all-purpose flour

1 quart (946 ml) chicken stock, store-bought or homemade

1 cup (150 g) chopped leftover smoked meat (preferably pork, but all meats are welcome here)

Kosher salt

1 bag (32 ounces, or 900 g) frozen crinkle-cut fries (I prefer Ore-Ida)

Meat Mitch Competition WHOMP! Rub, store-bought or homemade (see page 28)

1 package (1 pound, or 455 g) cheese curds (see Tips below)

½ cup (30 g) chopped fresh flat-leaf parsley (totally optional)

REAL MAN'S QUICHE WITH LUXURIOUS SMOKED MEATS

I know you've have had this moment: you opened up your refrigerator and there it was, leftover brisket, pork, ribs . . . you name it, it's there, and your partner is miffed because it's taking up all the space. Here is what you do to make everyone happy on a Sunday morning—make a quiche!

1 cup (235 ml) whole milk

1 cup (235 ml) heavy whipping cream

1 tablespoon (15 g) kosher salt

3 eggs

2¼ cup (248 g) shredded Swiss cheese

1 teaspoon kosher salt

Pinch of freshly ground black pepper

1 cup (150 g) assorted chopped smoked meats

1 deep dish frozen pie crust (Don't hate me, but I love the Pillsbury one.)

Combine the milk, cream, and salt in a large saucepan and heat over medium heat until scalded (meaning a skin begins to form on the surface). Remove from the heat and set aside to cool slightly, 10 to 15 minutes. Preheat the oven to 350°F (180°C).

Scatter the cheese and smoked meats evenly over the bottom of the pie crust. In a blender, mix the milk, cream, eggs, kosher salt, and pepper at full speed until nice and frothy, about 1 minute. Pour the mixture over the cheese and meats into the pie shell and carefully place in the oven. Don't spill it, Pods!

Bake the quiche for about 45 minutes or until slightly brown on top and the eggy custard is just set in the middle. Let it hang out in the pan until it's just warm, about 15 minutes longer. Cut into sixths and serve immediately

TIPS: Smoked bacon is a fine substitute, but cut the amount down to ½ cup (75 g) and maybe add some sauteed or smoked mushrooms or ½ cup (90 g) chopped and drained cooked spinach. You can also cool this completely, wrap, and either rewarm to serve or enjoy at room temperature with your favorite hot sauce.

Serves 6

BARBE-CUBAN SANDWICH

I love a great Cuban sandwich. One time, I spent day after day in Miami chasing the best one I could find. Enriqueta's Sandwich Shop rose above the rest. Their sandwich made me want to dance down the street. When you're making your own Cuban sandwich, you need to hit all the key flavors: pork, ham, Swiss cheese, mustard, and pickles. The bread is important, too—but it's hard to find the classic Cuban bread in most of the United States. So in this recipe, we'll make a loaf of store-bought Italian work. It might take a few tries to master the technique for pressing this sandwich, but once you get that press right, you'll have the ultimate sandwich!

Fire up a grill or warm a griddle or cast iron pan over medium heat.

Slice the loaf of bread in half lengthwise and flip so the cut side is facing up. On the inside, spread the yellow mustard on one side of the bread and the Char Bar Table Sauce on the other side. Layer the sandwich with half of the Swiss cheese first (this will act as the binder keeping the sandwich together), then pulled pork, deli ham, and dill pickles. Make sure to pat dry the pickle—we don't want them shooting out the sides! Finish with a top layer of cheese and then slap on the top piece of bread. Spread butter all over the outside of the sandwich and wrap completely in aluminum foil.

Place the sandwich on the grill or in the pan with the top-side down and press down with something heavy like a skillet or heavy plate—and no, sitting on it is not an option! The key here is to press the sandwiches and make them a nice even plank of deliciousness on both sides. I do 8 minutes per side for a nice golden crunch. You'll have a perfect sandwich when the cheese has melted and the meats are nice and warm on the inside.

Remove from the grill or skillet, remove the foil, cut into your choice of sandwich-size servings, and eat immediately!

Serves 6

1 loaf of Cuban or Italian bread

¼ cup (44 g) yellow mustard

¼ cup (66 g) Char Bar Table Sauce, store-bought or homemade (see page 29)

8 slices Swiss cheese

1 pound (455 g) smoked pulled pork (see Competition-Style Pulled Pork, page 51)

8 ounces (225 g) smoked deli ham, sliced

12 slices dill pickles, patted dry

2 tablespoons (28 g) unsalted butter

SMOKED BEEF CHEEK TACOS

Beef cheeks might sound scary, but don't be afraid! I see you reading this and saying to yourself, "No chance" . . . that's a mistake! Beef cheeks are as tender as your mother's pot roast, and this recipe takes them to another level. We're gonna add beer and hot sauce and make tacos that are ready for the road. Make them for tailgates, picnics, or impress your neighbors in the backyard because you know they're not smoking beef cheeks. Let's do this together!

3 pounds (1.4 kg) beef cheeks, trimmed of all silverskin, fat, and sinew

2 cups (384 g) Meat Mitch Steer Season Rub, store-bought or homemade (see page 31)

1 cup (235 ml) beef broth

1 can (12 ounces, or 355 ml) beer, preferably a Mexican lager such as Tecate

2 tablespoons (28 ml) Mexican hot sauce (I prefer Cholula or Valentina Mexican hot sauce)

1 yellow onion, sliced as thinly as possible

3 cloves garlic, peeled and smashed

12 corn tortillas

Salsa

½ cup (80 g) minced white onions

½ cup (8 g) chopped fresh cilantro

½ cup (60 g) grated cotija cheese

Set your smoker to 250°F (120°C) and get a good smoke rolling.

Toss the beef cheeks in the Meat Mitch Steer Season Rub, making sure to fully coat every inch of the cheek meat. Shake off any excess rub and place the beef cheeks on the grates, cover, and smoke for 2 hours or until the bark is set.

Put the cheeks in an aluminum pan with the beef broth, beer, hot sauce, onion, and garlic. Cover the pan with its lid or aluminum foil and return to the smoker or put in a 250°F (120°C, or gas mark ½) oven to continue to cook for 3 more hours.

Remove the pan from the smoker and let the meat rest for 20 minutes. When slightly cooled, shred the meat with two forks. Spoon some of the pan juices over the pulled meat, cover, and set aside while you prepare the tacos.

While the meat rests, wrap the corn tortillas in foil and set on the smoker to gently heat for 15 minutes. Remove the package from the smoker and place shredded meat on each tortilla. Top each taco with salsa, onion, cilantro, and cotija cheese and serve.

Makes 12 tacos

BRISKET ESQUITES SALAD

This killer side is inspired by *esquites*, aka Mexican street corn. There is a little prep work involved here because you have to husk and smoke the corn, but it's well worth it. I'm of the opinion that once you start throwing together smoked corn, brisket, cheese, citrus, garlic, mayo . . . OK, I'm stopping right there. My mouth is watering. Since this recipe takes some work, you can make life a little easier on yourself and prepare the dressing a day before the big party.

To make the Esquites Dressing, whisk together the mayonnaise, cheese, lime juice, and garlic in a mixing bowl. Using a rubber spatula, fold in the chili powder, tomato, green onions, cilantro, and serrano peppers. Cover and set aside in the refrigerator until you are ready to serve. (Any leftover dressing can be stored in a sealed container in the refrigerator for up to 7 days.)

To make the Roasted Corn, fire up the smoker to 250°F (120°C) and get a good smoke rolling. Chips are helpful to get as much smoke as possible in the box. While the smoker heats up, brush the corn with oil and season with salt and pepper. Smoke the corn for 1 hour, just enough to flavor the corn without cooking it too much. Then, lower the grates just over the coals and char the corn on all sides. (If your smoker can't do this, you can also transfer the corn to your grill to char.) Remove the corn from the smoker or grill and set aside.

When the corn is cool, cut the kernels off the cob into a large mixing bowl. Add the chopped brisket scraps. Add ½ cup (125 g) of the Esquites Dressing and mix with a rubber spatula. Taste for seasoning and add more dressing if you think it's needed. Serve immediately.

TIP: You can use frozen corn for this recipe. Get a cast iron skillet ripping hot and add 3 cups (492 g) of corn straight from the freezer bag. Let the corn char on one side in the dry skillet for about 1 minute. Let the corn cool and then combine the ingredients as you would with the corn cut from the cob.

Serves 8

ESQUITES DRESSING

½ cup (113 g) mayonnaise (I prefer Duke's)

1⅓ cup plus 1 tablespoon (170 g) cotija cheese, grated

3 tablespoons (45 ml) freshly squeezed lime juice

1 tablespoon (10 g) garlic minced to a fine paste

1 teaspoon chili powder

½ cup (90 g) seeded and chopped tomato

1 cup (100 g) thinly sliced green onions, green and white parts

½ cup (8 g) chopped fresh cilantro

2 serrano peppers, seeded and minced

ROASTED CORN

8 large ears of corn, husk and silk removed

¼ cup (60 ml) corn or vegetable oil

2 tablespoons (30 g) kosher salt

1 teaspoon freshly ground black pepper

1 cup (150 g) chopped leftover smoked brisket (see Competition-Style Beef Brisket and Burnt Ends, page 57)

SMOKED PORK CARNITAS

I love combining spice and smoke. This recipe does just that by marrying Mexican flavors like cumin, allspice, cinnamon, and citrus with more traditionally smoked barbecue meat. I think it's fun to mix it up and use the money muscle for something other than pulled pork sandwiches and meat platters! The keys to this dish are frying up the smoked pork in rich lard to make it extra porky and then finishing it with an easy salt blend that has bright citrus notes from real fruit. Find the best tortillas you can get your hands on, make (who are we kidding) or buy a great salsa, and make some killer carnitas tacos.

CARNITAS FINISHING SALT

1¼ cups (300 g) kosher salt

¼ cup (24 g) freshly ground black pepper

¼ cup (28 g) ground cumin

1 teaspoon ground allspice

1 teaspoon ground cinnamon

2 limes, zested on a microplane

1 orange, zested on a microplane

CARNITAS

¼ cup (56 g) lard or leftover pork fat drippings

2 pounds (900 g) smoked pork (see Competition-Style Pulled Pork, page 51), cooled and diced

Flour or corn tortillas, warmed, to serve

Salsa, to serve

Diced white onion, to serve

Chopped fresh cilantro, to serve

Preheat a large cast iron skillet or flat top to medium-high heat.

To make the Carnitas Finishing Salt, mix together the salt, black pepper, cumin, allspice, cinnamon, lime zest, and orange zest in a mixing bowl and then store in an airtight container. This makes a large batch and more than you need for this recipe, but it is one of those spice blends you'll be glad to have laying around. Try dusting other stuff you've cooked with it, even your favorite grilled veggies.

To make the Smoked Pork Carnitas, melt the lard in the hot skillet and add the diced smoked pork. Cook without moving or stirring until the pork begins to fry and crisp up on one side. Season with the Carnitas Finishing Salt and continue to cook for 30 seconds. With a spatula, stir the crispy pork to coat the back side of the meat and then transfer onto paper towel–lined plates. Serve immediately with freshly warmed tortillas, salsa, diced onions, and chopped cilantro.

Makes 12 to 16 delicious tacos

PIG CANDY

I love to say Pig Candy. You wouldn't have to tell me what it was and I would order it sight unseen. Bacon transcends all food groups and makes its own. This is an attempt to make a superhero even stronger . . . and at least for this episode, it flies! The salty, hammy, crunchy bacon takes on a sweet and spicy flavor that wakes up every corner of your mouth.

Set your smoker at 225°F (107°C) and get a good smoke rolling while we prepare these bad boys.

Lay out the bacon in a single layer on a baking sheet, nice and snug. We are just marinating for now. Drizzle about half the maple syrup over and spread into a very thin layer. Sprinkle some of the Meat Mitch Competition WHOMP! Rub over the bacon for a nice light coating. Flip the bacon over and repeat the process. Trust the process, my great buddy Gilly told me once!

The key to making Pig Candy is to smoke these hog planks on a wire rack so the fat can drip down and make the bacon nice and caramelized. Lay the bacon on a small wire rack that can fit on your smoker. Rub enough of the brown sugar on the bacon to lightly coat. Sprinkle half of the red pepper flakes over the bacon.

When your smoker is rolling, place the pork-laden wire rack in and close the door. Let her do her thing for an hour. Remove, flip the bacon pieces over, and sprinkle some more brown sugar and the rest of the red pepper flakes. Put the rack back in the smoker and finish cooking for at least another hour or until the bacon is nice and crispy.

Let rest at room temperature on the wire rack and then watch and see if the bacon actually gets up on its own and takes flight—it can happen.

TIP: See if you can get your bacon from the counter and skip the refrigerated package. That stuff has a ton of water injected into it and makes your Pig Candy less Superhuman. Get fired up, Jim!

Makes about 24 slices of Pig Candy, depending on how thick it's cut

2 pounds (900 g) thick-cut bacon from the deli counter or butcher shop (see Tip below)

1 cup (192 g) Meat Mitch Competition WHOMP! Rub, store-bought or homemade (see page 28)

½ cup (120 ml) real maple syrup

2 packed (450 g) cups light brown sugar

2 teaspoons crushed red pepper flakes

SMOKED BRISKET PHILLY CHEESESTEAK

I have stood on the corner of 9th Street and Passyunk Avenue in South Philly and stared down Pat's King of Steaks and Geno's Steaks. I admit I have held a face off (and eaten my face off) more than once. Here is a little homage to the home of cheesesteaks, and I promise you that you won't be disappointed. This sandwich is loaded with flavor and texture: gooey melted cheese, a crunchy toasted bun, and smoked crackly brisket. This is a favorite of my son, Will, and an all-time request from his buddies in the Mitchen.

2 yellow onions, diced

2 bell peppers (pick your colors), seeded and diced

Sliced mushrooms (optional)

3 pounds (1.4 kg) leftover smoked brisket (see Competition-Style Beef Brisket and Burnt Ends, page 57), cooled and diced

1 tablespoon (12 g) Meat Mitch Steer Season Rub, store-bought or homemade (see page 31)

1 can (8 ounces, or 225 g) Cheese Whiz

6 slices smoked provolone cheese

¾ cup (175 g) mayonnaise (I prefer Duke's)

6 hoagie rolls

Preheat a large cast iron skillet or flat top on your grill or stovetop over medium-high heat. When the pan is hot, add the onions, peppers, and mushrooms cook until the veggies char a little and soften up, 3 to 5 minutes, stirring if necessary.

Add the brisket and rub and cook for another 2 minutes to warm through. I like to bang on it with the side of my spatula like I'm doing a Hibachi-style cooking expo— loud and proud and breaking down that meat. Start squirting the Cheese Whiz at full squeeze. Quickly fold the melting cheese with the meat. Remove from the grill or from the heat. Stir, loosely cover, and set aside to let the cheese gently melt into the beef and veggies.

Spread the mayo over the inside of each roll. Heat a clean skillet over medium-high heat and toast the buns with the mayo-side down. Cook until just browned, about 30 seconds. Remove the lid from the brisket mixture and stir to fully incorporate the cheese and the meat.

Layer the bottom of each toasted roll with provolone cheese and then fill it up with the cheesy brisket mixture on top and serve immediately.

Makes 6 big sandwiches

CHIPPED SMOKED BEEF AND GRAVY (S.O.S.)

If you've never heard of S.O.S—sh*t on a shingle—it's the *best*! While you might have heard stories from your parents, there's a big difference between the low-end and classed-up versions of this dish. It's all about the richness of the high-quality smoked beef and the creaminess of homemade gravy. I've found the secret is getting the leftover beef really dry, almost like beef jerky. Trust me, it will work better with the gravy that way. Fry up enough eggs and this will be enough to serve four people an amazing breakfast.

To make the oven-dried chipped beef, preheat the oven to the lowest possible setting—at most 200°F (93°C, or gas mark ¼). Line a sheet pan with parchment paper.

Using two forks or your hands, shred the beef as finely as you can. Spread it out over the sheet pan and dry it in the oven for 3 to 4 hours or until dry and crispy without over-browning. Remove from the oven and spread it out to continue to dry on paper towel-lined plates. Stir after 90 minutes and continue to dry.

To make the gravy, heat the canola oil in a saucepan over medium heat. Add the oven-dried beef and sauté for about 2 minutes. While the beef cooks, mix the flour and water in a medium-sized bowl with a whisk or fork until there are no lumps. Add the flour and water mixture to the sautéed beef and stir, continuing to cook over medium heat for about 5 minutes. It should noticeably thicken. Add the milk, increase the heat to medium-high, and bring the mixture to a boil. Immediately turn down the heat to medium-low heat and simmer for about 10 minutes. While the gravy simmers, get the biscuits ready by warming them up or, if using toast, toast the bread slices to your liking in a toaster or toaster oven. Butter the toast and place on four plates. When the gravy is done cooking, cover the biscuits or toast with the gravy and serve immediately.

Serves 4

1 pound (455 g) leftover smoked brisket (see Competition-Style Beef Brisket and Burnt Ends, page 57)

2 tablespoons (28 ml) canola oil

¼ cup (31 g) all-purpose flour

1 cup (235 ml) water

1 cup (235 ml) milk

2 biscuits, cut in half, or 4 slices sourdough or wheat bread

Unsalted butter

BURNT END GRILLED CHEESE

Kansas City is known for our burnt ends, crispy and crusty bite-size pieces of succulent brisket points that explode in your mouth. Sure, some might want to enjoy them only straight-up, but I say don't listen to anyone that says you can't eat them with cheese! This is a warm and slightly spicy sando that you just shove into your face and don't bother opening your mouth. I like to spice this sandwich up with a mixture of peppery cheese and the kick of my Meat Mitch Competition WHOMP! BBQ Sauce, but feel free to choose your own adventure.

8 slices sourdough bread

2 tablespoons (28 g) mayonnaise (I prefer Duke's)

4 slices best cheddar you can find (We love the local brand Boulevard Tank 7 Cheddar)

4 slices Ghost Pepper Colby Jack or any hot pepper cheese

1 pound (455 g) diced burnt ends (see Competition-Style Beef Brisket and Burnt Ends, page 57), warm

Meat Mitch Competition WHOMP! BBQ Sauce, store-bought or homemade (see page 32)

Heat your charcoal or gas grill to medium-low heat. The key here is to get the sandwich nice 'n' toasty and not burned.

Thinly spread one side of each bread slice with mayonnaise. Place the bread, mayonnaise-side down, on the grill. Place 1 slice of cheddar on top of half of the slices and 1 slice of Ghost Pepper Colby Jack on the remaining pieces. Spoon one-quarter of the warm burnt ends onto the cheddar cheese slices and, using tongs, place the Ghost Pepper Colby Jack–topped bread on top of the meat.

Gently press the sandwiches and then rotate 90 degrees after 2 minutes. Grill another 2 minutes and then gently flip the sandwiches to the other side. Cook this side just like you did the first side. If the sandwich is not heated through and the cheese isn't melted, continue to flip and cook the sandwich until it's oozing, and you want to eat it straight off the grill. This is when I hit it with a little BBQ sauce!

Let the sandwiches cool on a wire rack for 1 minute before serving as we don't want to melt your taste buds.

TIPS: Feel free to have fun with other types of bread, like marble rye and Texas toast. We love making these with other meats as well. Smoked turkey on this sandwich makes a killer lunchtime meal!

Serves 4

MATT PITTMAN

MEAT CHURCH BBQ
WAXAHACHIE, TEXAS

I first saw Matt Pittman on TV several years ago, competing in the extremely popular *BBQ Pitmasters* show. The show challenges three regional pitmasters to compete against each other in different categories until they determine a winner. Matt didn't win that competition but he did declare himself the winner of the Best Hair in BBQ. (I thought I could compete with the meats, but stood no shot with the hair!)

What Matt has accomplished since that show has been remarkable. We met shortly thereafter at The American Royal World Series of Barbecue competition in Kansas City and became fast friends. Throughout the years, we would regularly talk about the BBQ industry, developing products, marketing products, competing—you name it. He launched his own line of Meat Church BBQ rubs and seasonings, which have catapulted him to huge success. We both had long-standing careers in other fields and dreamed of one day going all-in and chasing our barbecue dreams. Fortunately, we both made the leap. I am in awe of the success he has experienced and the trail he has blazed to become a top spokesman in barbecue. I am so thankful for his friendship, help, advice, and loyalty. He has honed his craft and raised his level of competition on all fronts to where he is truly elite—and I am still jealous of his hair!

PORK BELLY BURNT ENDS

RECIPE BY MATT PITTMAN, PHOTO ON PAGE 173

The internet is full of pictures and rhetoric surrounding the ever-popular pork belly burnt ends. Purists scream that you can't make burnt ends this way because it isn't made with brisket, and it shouldn't be labeled as such. All I scream is that I love it and want more! Matt has led the charge with this recipe and fortunately for me, he believes that his famous recipe goes best with Meat Mitch WHOMP! Naked BBQ Sauce! This is basically for bacon lovers because it tastes like crispy bite-sized chunks of bacon that explode with salty sweet flavor. You end up just standing there and popping them in your mouth. When someone comes near your pan of these love morsels, you'll go into complete NBA box-out mode—eat them fast!

1 skinless pork belly, about 5 pounds (2.3 kg)

Apple juice, for spritzing

2 cups (576 g) Meat Church Honey Hog Rub, Meat Church Honey Hog BBQ Rub, or Meat Church The Gospel All-Purpose Rub (see Tip below)

1 bottle (21 ounces, or 595 g) Meat Mitch WHOMP! Naked BBQ Sauce

1 jar (12 ounces, or 340 g) clover honey

Set your smoker to 275°F (140°C) and get a good smoke rolling. I recommend a medium smoke wood for this cook, such as hickory or pecan.

Using a sharp, big boy knife, cube the pork belly into 1-inch (5 cm) cubes. Thoroughly coat all sides of the pork belly cubes with your choice of rub (you won't use all of it). Allow the rub to adhere on all sides for at least 15 minutes.

Place the pork belly on a wire rack in the smoker fat-side up. This cook will take 3 hours. Spritz the pork belly with apple juice every 45 minutes or whenever it starts to look dry. Using your digital probe thermometer, pull the belly when the meat reaches an internal temperature of 190 to 195°F (88 to 90.5°C). Some people pull their belly a lot earlier, but I want it really tender!

Place the cubes in a large roasting pan. Season and toss the cubes with the remaining rub. Cover the cubes with the BBQ sauce. Drizzle the honey across the top. Finally, toss the cubes thoroughly to ensure they are completely covered.

Return the pan, uncovered, to the smoker and cook for another hour or until all liquid has reduced and caramelized. Allow to cool for 15 minutes and enjoy!

TIP: Meat Church products can be purchased online at meatchurch.com. You can even use Meat Church Holy Gospel BBQ Rub or Honey Hog Hot BBQ Rub. These are spicier rubs, which is what I prefer because I finish these with a sweet sauce.

Makes about 3 pounds (1.4 kg)

MEAT CHURCH'S SMOKED BOLOGNA

RECIPE BY MATT PITTMAN

My bologna has a first name and its S-M-O-K-E-D! There is no better way to have it. This takes your childhood lunch program straight to a NASA takeoff mission. It's a fan favorite and with the scoring, it becomes visually stunning. You'll get some skeptical smiles when you tell your friends what you're smoking and lots of empty plates when you are done serving them!

Set your smoker to 250°F (120°C) and get a good smoke rolling. We recommend a medium smoke wood or pellet for this cook, such as hickory or pecan, but any wood will do.

Using your sharpest knife, score the chub. Slice a small incision about ½ inch (1 cm)- deep down the length of the chub and repeat around the entire chub, spacing the cuts approximately 1 inch (5 cm) apart. This will open up the bologna as it cooks, giving more surface area for seasoning and smoke. (Plus, it reminds me of how my Granny prepared her slices.)

Slather the chub completely with yellow mustard to act as a binder for the seasoning. Otherwise, it's really difficult to get the seasoning to adhere. This won't affect the flavor profile and your final product will not taste like mustard. Season liberally with the Meat Church The Gospel All-Purpose Rub.

Place the chub in your smoker. Smoke for at least 2 hours. Some folks like to go longer. Time is not super important on this cook as you are simply reheating a cooked piece of meat and trying to impart some smoke flavor into it.

Remove the chub from the smoker. Allow to cool for 10 minutes.

Slice ¼-inch (6 mm) thick. Sear in a piping hot cast iron skillet for 45 seconds per side. Serve in sandwiches with any ingredients you like!

TIPS: Bologna chubs—big cylinders of bologna—can be purchased at delis as well as some Sam's Clubs and Costco locations. Meat Church products can be purchased online at meatchurch.com.

Makes enough bologna for at least 20 sandwiches

5-pound (2.3 kg) chub unsliced bologna (see Tips below), unwrapped

1 teaspoon yellow mustard

Meat Church The Gospel All-Purpose BBQ Rub (see Tips below)

Sandwich fixings, to serve

SMOKED QUESO

RECIPE BY MATT PITTMAN

Try this rich blend of real man's cheese, sausage, tomatoes, and creamy soup all mixed together and highlighted by Matt's tantalizingly spicy Holy Voodoo rub. This is a new go-to appetizer and crowd pleaser! You can also get crazy with the mix-ins. I have personally substituted various shellfish such as scallops, shrimp, crab, and lobster and it was amazing, but save that treatment for good friends because it can be heavy on the wallet.

2 16-ounce (453 g) tubes hot (spicy) breakfast sausage (such as Jimmy Dean sausage rolls)

2-pound (900 g) block Velveeta cheese (Don't try to go cheap with a generic alternative.)

16 ounces (455 g) smoked Gouda

2 cans (10 ounces, or 280 g each) Rotel tomatoes

1 can (10.5 ounces, or 295 g) cream of mushroom soup (see Tips below)

2 tablespoons (36 g) Meat Church Holy Voodoo Seasoning (see Tips below)

½ cup (8 g) chopped fresh cilantro

Set your smoker to 350°F (180°C) and get a good smoke rolling. We like a heavy smoke wood such as oak, mesquite, or hickory for this cook since it won't be in the smoker long.

Heat a Dutch oven over medium-high heat, crumble in the sausage, and cook for 8 minutes until the sausage is browned. Drain the fat off.

Slice the Velveeta into 1-inch (5 cm) slices and cube the Gouda into 1-inch (5 cm) squares. Add them to the sausage in the Dutch oven. Then, add the canned tomatoes with their liquid and the cream of mushroom soup. Add the Meat Church Holy Voodoo Seasoning.

Place the Dutch oven, uncovered, in your smoker and smoke for 45 minutes, stirring 3 to 4 times during the cook. Add most of the cilantro during the last 5 minutes of the cook, saving a little for garnish at the end.

Allow to cool slightly, garnish with the remaining cilantro, and enjoy!

TIPS: Substitute cream of whatever soup you like for the cream of mushroom soup. Cream of chicken soup works well. Meat Church products can be purchased online at meatchurch.com.

Makes about 4 cups (832 g) smoky, creamy queso

CHORIZO JALAPEÑO POPPERS

RECIPE BY MATT PITTMAN

Jalapeño poppers are easily one of the most popular appetizers found on smokers during every competition. They are fun to make, not too messy to eat on the fly as you walk around, and so damn delicious. In this recipe, Matt blends spicy chorizo with an already hot jalapeño and then cools you back down with cream cheese and salty bacon. Matt adds his famous Honey Hog BBQ Rub, which leaves some sweetness on your lips from this well-rounded appetizer.

Set the smoker to 275°F (140°C) and get a good smoke rolling. We like hickory or pecan wood for this smoke.

To prepare the stuffing, heat a skillet over medium heat. Add the chorizo and fry until it is fully cooked. Drain off the fat. Immediately mix the chorizo and cream cheese together in a small bowl. The warm chorizo will help soften the cream cheese. Add the Meat Church Honey Hog BBQ Rub to taste, mix well, and set aside.

Cut off the stem and core each jalapeño. Slice them in half and remove all of the seeds. Leave the membranes if you want them hotter. Fill each jalapeño up with the cream cheese mixture. Wrap each jalapeño with a ½ slice of bacon. A toothpick won't be required as long as you didn't use massive peppers. Dust the tops of the jalapeño poppers with more rub seasoning and, if you like, top the poppers with cracked black pepper.

Smoke the peppers for 60 to 90 minutes until the bacon looks perfect! Cool for 10 to 15 minutes and then enjoy one of our favorite appetizers!

TIP: Meat Church products can be purchased online at meatchurch.com.

Makes 32 portions of spicy, gooey goodness

10 ounces (280 g) fresh Mexican chorizo

8 ounces (225 g) cream cheese

2 tablespoons (36 g) Meat Church Honey Hog BBQ Rub (or use Meat Church The Gospel All-Purpose Rub or Meat Church Deez Nuts Honey Pecan BBQ Rub), plus more to taste

16 jalapeños (not too large, so the bacon wraps around nicely)

1 package (12 ounces, or 340 g) standard-cut bacon (thick-cut bacon doesn't work as well)

Cracked black pepper (optional)

5

SIDES, DESSERTS, AND OTHER DELIGHTS FROM THE "MITCHEN"

It is demoralizing to spend 12 hours smoking a killer brisket only to sit around the table and hear continuous raves about your neighbor Suzy's three bean salad. Don't forget: sides can be showstopping! In this chapter, I'll take you on a tour of dishes that you can make, serve, and wait for the compliments to roll in. You'll find an addictive pimento cheese recipe along with a delicious spin on deviled eggs. And get ready to knock BBQ beans and potatoes out of the park!

Do you have a sweet tooth? I do. Thankfully, so does my daughter, Piper. She can make a whoopie pie sing and a chocolate chip cookie taste like it's the first time you ever had one. Whether it's blueberries or strawberries, we have something that will make you come back for seconds.

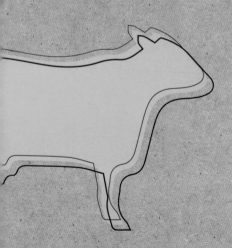

CRACK PIMENTO CHEESE WITH TOASTED BLACK PEPPERCORNS

So, I moved over to Paris to help open a BBQ restaurant and centered everything around toasting and grinding black peppercorns—they completely open up like a walk through Times Square during Christmas. The aroma stands you up and makes you pay attention. Many have done it before me, but I honestly believe it changes the entire dynamic of this amazingly simple pimento cheese. This is a traditional, easy Southern recipe with few ingredients, but it has *everything* I need. I have made it a million times for family and friends, and it has quickly become one of the most requested!

To make the pimentos, grill the red peppers over high heat or roast them in the oven to char the outside. I often throw them right on top of the grates of my gas stove. Place in a zip top storage bag or in a large, sealable container and let steam until cool. When the peppers are cool, peel, rinse, seed, and finely dice them. Let soak in the vinegar at room temperature for as long as you can—preferably overnight. Cover and refrigerate until you are ready to use.

To make the Pimento Cheese, mix together the onion, ground toasted peppercorns, salt, mayonnaise, and hot sauce in a large mixing bowl. Add the cheeses and stir to combine. Add the homemade pimentos and all of the vinegar and mix until combined. Taste for seasoning and adjust with salt if needed.

Keep cold in the refrigerator until you are ready to serve.

Makes about 3 cups (720 g)

HOMEMADE PIMENTOS

2 red bell peppers

¼ cup (60 ml) apple cider vinegar

PIMENTO CHEESE

1 tablespoon (10 g) finely grated red onion

½ tablespoon (or more) of ground toasted black peppercorns (see below)

¼ teaspoon kosher salt

2 cups (450 g) mayonnaise (I prefer Duke's)

1½ teaspoons hot sauce

1 pound (455 g) aged yellow cheddar cheese (I recommend Tillamook), grated

½ pound (225 g) aged white cheddar cheese, grated

HOW TO TOAST PEPPERCORNS

Cover the entire bottom of a small non-stick pan with a single layer of peppercorns.

Toast over medium heat for about 4 to 5 minutes until you smell an intense peppery aroma. Think about the times you've smelled freshly roasted nuts, or maybe you've toasted other spices . . . the smell is noticeable!

Once you hear some of the peppercorns crack and snap, turn off the heat and transfer the peppercorns to a bowl to cool. Add cooled peppercorns to a pepper grinder or coffee grinder to grind coarsely.

TAILGATE BBQ BEANS

Don't buy canned baked beans—this recipe is too easy and too good! I bet you have most of these ingredients already in your kitchen. It's time to throw them all together along with the smoked meat you slaved over all weekend. Let's make some beans!! These beans are sweet with just a touch of heat—isn't that everyone's motto? Molasses, brown sugar, Char Bar Table Sauce, smoked meat . . . really?! True to Kansas City, these BBQ Beans will keep your tailgate going long after the game.

1 tablespoon (14 g) bacon drippings

2 yellow onions, minced

1 green bell pepper, minced

6 garlic cloves, minced

1 tablespoon (12 g) Meat Mitch Steer Season Rub, store-bought or homemade (see page 29)

2 teaspoons dried oregano

1 tablespoon (6 g) freshly ground black pepper

¼ teaspoon chili powder

2 cups (528 g) Char Bar Table Sauce, store-bought or homemade (see page 29) (see Tip below)

¼ cup (44 g) yellow mustard

½ cup (115 g) packed dark brown sugar

½ cup (170 g) light molasses

8 ounces (225 g) leftover smoked meat, preferably beef and pork, chopped

5 cans (15 ounces, or 425 g each) pinto beans, drained and rinsed

Grab a big ol' pot and melt the delicious bacon fat over medium heat until hot. Add the onions and green bell peppers, turn the heat to medium-low, and cook for 20 minutes. Add the garlic, cover, and continue to cook for another 10 minutes or so, or until it reaches your desired thickness.

Add the Meat Mitch Steer Season Rub, oregano, black pepper, chili powder, Char Bar Table Sauce, mustard, brown sugar, and molasses. Stir to get it all mixed up. Then, add the chopped meats and all of the beans. Stir it up like Bob Marley and bring to a simmer. Cover and continue to simmer for 10 more minutes with the lid on.

Remove the lid and taste the mix. Adjust for seasoning and reduce with the lid off if there's too much liquid. Serve when you have it just right or cool down and just rewarm it when the game starts!

TIP: Char Bar Table Sauce is obviously the best Kansas City–style barbecue sauce on the planet and it gives this chili that extra touch of heat. But in case you don't have any on hand, or don't want to make any, you can always use whatever Kansas City–style sauce is in the fridge. C'mon, Pods.

Makes about 2 quarts (1.9 L)

MY MOM'S POTATO SALAD

My mom didn't cook often. There is a reason for that. Because once she started, you never knew what you were going to get. Most often, it didn't work out: like the time she put a can of black bean dip into the spaghetti sauce because she was out of hamburger. With this recipe, however, she got it right every time! It's a creamy mayonnaise-based salad with just enough vinegar for balance. Celery adds some crunch and there's a good amount of mustard flavor as well. Sure, she didn't use my signature Meat Mitch Competition WHOMP! Rub, but I sure do. Most people like their potato salad cold, but try this one warm as well—I love it that way!

Fill a large stockpot with water. Season liberally with kosher salt. The water should taste like the ocean. Add the diced potatoes and bring to a boil. Turn down to a simmer and cook until tender, but not falling apart, about 30 minutes.

While the potatoes are cooking, combine the mayonnaise, sour cream, whole-grain mustard, Dijon mustard, pickle relish, buttermilk, rub, horseradish, vinegar, salt, and white pepper in a large mixing bowl and stir to completely mix. Add the celery, hard-boiled eggs, and green onions and mix completely again.

When potatoes are cooked, drain in a colander. Let the potatoes the cool slightly and then mix the warm potatoes into the dressing. Serve warm or allow to cool completely and then chill. Serve with your favorite main dish from the smoker.

Makes about 16 servings

- 4 large russet potatoes, peeled and diced
- 2 cups (450 g) mayonnaise (I prefer Duke's)
- ¼ cup (60 g) sour cream
- 5 teaspoons (25 g) whole-grain mustard
- ¼ cup (60 g) Dijon mustard
- 3 tablespoons (45 g) dill pickle relish
- ¼ cup (60 ml) buttermilk
- ¾ teaspoon Meat Mitch Competition WHOMP! Rub, store-bought or homemade (see page 28)
- 1½ teaspoons prepared horseradish
- ¾ teaspoons red wine vinegar
- ½ teaspoons kosher salt
- ⅛ teaspoon white pepper
- 4 stalks celery, thinly sliced
- 4 hard-boiled eggs, diced
- ¼ cup (25 g) thinly sliced green onions, white and green parts

CHARRED SOUS VIDE CAULIFLOWER STEAKS

Sous vide? Sous you! It's crazy that a machine that was expensive and only found in high-end kitchens not long ago is now almost as accessible as a slow cooker. You can even find it at some big-box stores! Simply put, sous vide is the process of putting food in a vacuum-sealed bag and cooking in a large pot of water that is held at a set temperature. The result is perfectly cooked meats, vegetables, fish, and eggs (well, perfect once you get your time and temperatures locked in). For this recipe, cauliflower takes a bath and becomes incredibly silky and tender. You can finish it on the grill or use a cast iron skillet to char and crisp up the florets. Those charred flavors and the crunch contrast with the soft interior of the cauliflower . . . and you know what I dig: that vibrant yellow color from the saffron. Pair it with champagne and oysters for a fancy night in.

1 large head cauliflower

4 cloves garlic, smashed

1 cup (235 ml) extra virgin olive oil

1 teaspoon crumbled saffron threads

1 teaspoon ground coriander

4 teaspoons (20 g) kosher salt

1 teaspoon freshly ground black pepper

1 lemon, halved

Chopped fresh flat-leaf parsley, to garnish

Prepare your water bath in the sous vide and set your circulator to 185°F (85°C).

To cut the cauliflower into steaks, place the cauliflower on your cutting board with the stem-side down. Carefully cut ⅛ inch (3 mm) off each side. Make one cut down the middle of the plant and then one cut down the middle of each of the two pieces.

While the water heats, put the garlic in a small saucepan with the olive oil. Cook over medium heat until the garlic begins to brown, about 3 minutes. Remove the pan from the heat and add the saffron. Let it steep for 15 minutes and then strain the mixture through a fine-mesh strainer. Let the oil cool completely.

Place each cauliflower steak in its own sealable plastic bag and add ¼ teaspoon of the ground coriander, 1 teaspoon of the salt, and 1 teaspoon of the black pepper. Add ¼ cup (60 ml) of the saffron oil to each bag and seal according to the manufacturer's directions. Place all the bags in the preheated water bath and cook for 1 hour. After the hour is up, remove the bags and let cool to room temperature.

While the cauliflower cools, fire up a charcoal or gas grill to high heat or preheat a cast iron skillet over high heat. Cut open the bags and remove the cauliflower steaks. Using metal tongs, place the steaks on the grill or skillet and cook until lightly charred on both sides. Put 1 to 2 steaks on each plate and squeeze lemon juice over the cauliflower. Garnish with the chopped parsley and serve immediately.

Makes plenty for 4 to share as a side, or serve as a main for 2

STAND-UP DEVILED EGGS

If it's Easter, Thanksgiving, Christmas, Halloween, you name it—you are asked to bring something. I am telling you right now, you will be hard pressed to bring something more fun, interactive, visually cool, and delicious than these eggs—if you bring them with all the fixings! An egg is an egg is an egg. I was taught that in college, somehow. I think it had to do with us breaking into the kitchen late night and ravaging the fridge. Where I am going with this is where the egg is the focus, looks cool standing up, and holds more filling, but all the fun happens with what you throw on top. It's a party! Build an egg bar—everyone will pack around these creamy, silky bites of heaven!

Fill a large pot about halfway up with water and bring to a boil. Using a large slotted spoon or strainer, gently lower the eggs straight from the fridge into the boiling water. Set a timer for 11 minutes and turn the heat down just to the slightest simmer. Cover the pot and prepare a large bowl with lots of ice and a little cold water to shock the eggs.

When the timer goes off, drain the eggs and immediately plop them in the icy water. If a couple of them have cracked open, it's okay! They'll still be great. Let them completely cool in the bath for at least 20 minutes. The eggs should peel easily. Make sure you rinse any bits of shell off and then pat them dry with a paper towel.

Using a sharp paring knife, nick just enough of one end of the egg so that it can stand up. On the other side of the egg, slice through it about two-thirds of the way down, or enough to where you can dig out all of the yolk. Dig out all of the yolks and put the whites aside. Put the yolks in a mixing bowl with the mustard, garlic, Tabasco, salt, and pepper. Mash it all up with a fork until a smooth paste forms. Fold in the mayonnaise and green onions and taste to make sure it's where you want it.

Spoon the mix back into the egg whites, stand 'em up on the side you snipped, and dust with the Old Bay Seasoning. Put your accompaniments in ramekins. Watch your friends and family top their eggs with all the amazing sides from the bar and walk around it barking out, "Egg Bar, Pods! We got Eggs! Amazing Eggs!"

Serves 12

1 dozen large eggs

2 teaspoons Dijon mustard

1 garlic clove, finely grated on a microplane

1 teaspoon Tabasco sauce

½ teaspoon freshly ground black pepper

¾ teaspoon kosher salt

6 tablespoons (120 g) mayonnaise (I prefer Duke's)

2 tablespoons (12 g) thinly sliced green onions, white and green parts

½ teaspoon Old Bay Seasoning

Pig Candy (see page 165), caviar, Pickled Onions (see page 154), chopped sundried tomatoes, kalamata olives, rinsed capers, smoked salmon, diced fresh tomatoes, and anything else you'd like at your deviled egg bar

WHOOPIE PIES

This recipe is near and dear to my stomach and also my wife. Her Nan used to make these to perfection and we all loved her very much. We would bet every year on the World Series and I would take payment in the pies! We would also travel for these bad boys. Every year, we make the journey with our kids from Kansas City to the Jersey Shore, where we stay with family on the water. This is my favorite week (sometimes two) of the year. Without fail, whoopie pies are made and tucked inside coolers along with adult beverages for our day on the beach. The original whoopie pie was chocolate cake cookies with vanilla cream, but now there are all sorts of flavors—there are entire cookbooks devoted to them! They are unquestionably our family's favorite and also a favorite among the many seagulls, as they will stop at nothing to dive bomb their beaks into these handheld chocolatey treasures.

OUTSIDE COOKIES

1 cup (2 sticks, or 225 g) unsalted butter, softened

2 cups (400 g) granulated white sugar

2 large eggs

1 teaspoon vanilla extract

1 cup (235 ml) whole milk

1 tablespoon (15 ml) white vinegar

4½ cups (563 g) all-purpose flour

1 cup (80 g) unsweetened cocoa powder

2 teaspoons table salt

1 cup (235 ml) water

2 teaspoons baking soda

CREAM FILLING

2 egg whites

1 tablespoon (15 ml) vanilla extract

4 tablespoons (31 g) all-purpose flour

4 cups (480 g) confectioners' sugar

1½ cups (300 g) Crisco vegetable shortening

To make the cookies, preheat the oven to 350°F (180°C, or gas mark 4). Line four half-sheet pans with parchment paper and spray with nonstick cooking spray.

In a stand mixer fitted with the paddle attachment, beat the softened butter and white sugar until light and fluffy. Beat in the eggs and vanilla on medium speed until incorporated.

In a separate bowl, mix the milk and vinegar and let sit for 10 minutes to sour. Add to the creamed butter mixture and beat until incorporated.

Add the flour, cocoa, table salt, and ¾ cup (175 ml) of the water and mix over medium speed, making sure not to overmix, about 1 minute. In a small bowl, mix the remaining ¼ cup (60 ml) of water and baking soda and add to the stand mixer bowl. Mix everything just to blend.

Drop 6 individual 2-ounce (¼ cup, or 60 ml) scoops onto each prepared pan, spacing evenly. Bake two sheets at a time for 12 minutes, rotating the pans every 3 minutes. Remove the cookies from the hot sheet pans to cooling racks and cool completely.

To make the filling, in the bowl of a stand mixer fitted with the whisk attachment, combine the egg whites, vanilla, flour, confectioners' sugar, and vegetable shortening and beat over low speed for 1 minute. Increase the speed to medium-high and beat until fluffy, about 5 minutes.

Fill each pair of the cookies with 2 tablespoons (28 ml) of the filling, wrap in plastic wrap, and refrigerate until you are ready to serve.

Makes 24 Whoopie Pies

BLUEBERRY HAND PIES

Ah, hand pies. When it comes to this recipe, and many other desserts, the talented Julia Haberer inspired and taught my daughter how to make it. She made these for a big dinner where I served up smoked lamb chops. I worked so hard on those chops and everyone just talked about these damn hand pies! I can see why, though. The crust reminds me of my grandmother's, and they are just packed full of blueberries. Good thing everyone gets their own because nobody wants to share them!

To make the crust, combine the sour cream, lemon juice, and ice water in a small bowl and set aside.

In a food processor, combine the flour, salt, and granulated sugar. With the food processor running, chuck little pieces of the butter in one at a time and pulse until it all resembles a coarse meal. Gradually add the sour cream mixture and pulse just until combined. The mixture will be crumbly. Test by pinching a small amount of dough together to see if it holds. If it does not hold together, pulse in more water, 1 teaspoon at a time, until it holds together. Divide the dough in half and press into two flat rectangles. Grab your plastic wrap, wrap it up, and refrigerate until firm, around an hour or so.

Meanwhile, make the filling. Get the blueberries ready for action by placing them in a medium-size bowl and mixing them with the white sugar, cornstarch, and lemon zest. Gently stir together until the mixture is well combined. Set aside.

To assemble the hand pies, get the dough out of the refrigerator and let it hang out on the counter for about 10 minutes before rolling. Throw a little flour on a piece of parchment paper and set aside. Using a flour-dusted rolling pin, roll out the dough on the counter until it's about ¼ inch (6 mm)-thick, adding more flour as needed. Cut the dough into 4½-inch (11 cm) rounds, placing the cut pieces on the parchment. You should find yourself with about 16 dough circles in all.

Mound 1 heaping tablespoon (15 ml) of the berry mixture in the center of each dough circle. Brush the edges of the dough with the egg and fold the top halves over the fruit to enclose. Press firmly around the edges with a fork to seal. With a sharp knife, cut a steam vent in each pie. Place the pies 2 inches (5 cm) apart on the lined baking sheets. Transfer the unbaked pies to the freezer and let chill for 15 minutes until slightly firm.

While the pies chill, preheat the oven to 375°F (190°C, or gas mark 5), with the oven racks in the upper and lower thirds of the oven.

Remover the pies from the freezer and lightly brush with the remaining egg wash. Sprinkle with the sanding sugar.

Bake for about 35 minutes until lightly browned, rotating the sheets and switching from top and bottom halfway through. Transfer to a wire rack to cool. It's time to eat! (Just make sure you don't get too greedy and eat too soon. I don't want you to burn your mouth!) These eat just as good at room temperature.

Makes 16 Blueberry Hand Pies

CRUST

1 tablespoon (15 g) sour cream

1 tablespoon (15 ml) lemon juice

2 tablespoons (28 ml) ice water, plus extra if needed

1¼ cups (156 g) all-purpose flour, plus more for rolling

½ teaspoon kosher salt

1 teaspoon granulated white sugar

½ cup (1 stick, or 112 g) unsalted butter, cut into small pieces and chilled

FILLING

⅓ cup (67 g) granulated white sugar

1½ cups (233 g) frozen blueberries

1 tablespoon (6 g) lemon zest

4½ teaspoons (12 g) cornstarch

TOPPING

1 large egg, lightly beaten

Sanding sugar or turbinado sugar, for sprinkling

STRAWBERRY TOASTER PASTRIES

RECIPE BY PIPER BENJAMIN

When I found out that we could actually make our own toaster pastries, I thought my daughter was teasing me. Piper has taken the pop out of these pastries and has replaced it with a bang! They are packed with strawberries upon strawberries inside a wonderful crust that provides a firm bite, but then the strawberries run through your mouth like a jailbreak. As for the icing, can I just tell you I understand the saying "like icing on a cake." It is just devilishly good and colorful—makes it all worthwhile. Admittedly, there is work that goes into this perfection—if you want easy, get the box—but it's not even close to being the same.

CRUST

2 tablespoons (30 g) sour cream

2 tablespoons (28 ml) freshly squeezed lemon juice

4 tablespoons (60 ml) ice water, plus extra if needed

2½ cups (313 g) all-purpose flour, plus more for rolling

1 teaspoon kosher salt

2 teaspoons granulated sugar

1 cup (2 sticks, or 225 g) unsalted butter, chilled

FILLING

½ cup (100 g) granulated sugar

1 cup (145 g) fresh strawberries

2 tablespoons (28 ml) freshly squeezed lemon juice

1 tablespoon (8 g) cornstarch

To make the crust, mix the sour cream, lemon juice and ice water in a small bowl. Set aside.

In food processor, combine the flour, salt, and sugar and buzz up until well mixed, maybe 6 or 7 pulses. Chuck all of the cold butter pieces in and keep pulsing until the mixture looks nice and crumbly, 10 to 12 more pulses. Add the sour cream mixture and mix it all up just until combined. The mixture should still be crumbly. Test by pinching a small amount of dough together to see if it holds. If it does not hold together, add more water, 1 teaspoon at a time until it holds together. Divide the dough in half and press into two rectangles. Wrap each in plastic wrap and refrigerate until firm, about 1 hour.

To make the filling, combine the granulated sugar, strawberries, lemon juice, and cornstarch in a saucepan over medium heat. Allow the mixture to come to a simmer and then use an immersion blender or potato masher to blend to a semi-smooth jam-like consistency, allowing some chunks of fruit to remain. Be careful to do all this slowly, so you don't burn yourself!

Simmer the filling for 20 minutes or until the mixture has thickened. Cool completely before you use it in the toaster pastries. It's best to refrigerate overnight, but it can work when fully chilled after 2 hours in the refrigerator.

To make the toaster pastries, preheat the oven to 375°F (190°C, or gas mark 5) with racks in the upper and lower thirds of the oven. Line a baking sheet with parchment paper. Remove the dough from the refrigerator and allow it to rest at room temperature for about 10 minutes.

Throw a little flour on a piece of parchment paper and spread it all over. Using a flour dusted rolling pin, roll out the dough and cut it into 3-inch by 4-inch (7.5 cm by 10 cm) rectangles. Arrange the dough rectangles into two rows. Prick the top row with a fork, five to six times, which allows steam to be released and keeps the toaster pastry from turning into a soggy mess.

Lightly brush all four edges of the bottom rectangles with the remaining egg wash. Scoop 1 heaping tablespoon (15 ml) of filling onto the center of bottom rectangles. Lay the top pastry over the filling and use your fingers to firmly press the top and bottom together. Place the pastries 1 to 2 inches (2.5 to 5 cm) apart on the prepared baking sheet.

Get out your handy pastry brush and lightly coat the pastries with egg wash. Bake, rotating the sheets and switching racks halfway through, for about 25 minutes, until the pastries are golden brown. Transfer to a wire rack to cool completely.

While the pastries are cooling, make the icing. Combine the egg whites and vanilla in a stand mixer fitted with the whip attachment and beat until frothy. Add the confectioners' sugar gradually and mix on low speed until incorporated. Beat on high until mixture is glossy, about 5 to 6 minutes. With a big spatula, spread the icing all over the cooled pastries.

Allow the icing to dry on the pastries, uncovered, overnight. Serve the next day and become everyone's new best friend.

TIP: Get crazy with sprinkles, nuts, candy—really anything you like that will stick to the icing. Just make sure you get it all on the icing before it dries or it won't stick.

Makes 8 pastries

photo on following page

EGG WASH

2 large egg, lightly beaten

ICING

2 large egg whites

1 teaspoon vanilla extract

2½ cups (300 g) confectioners' sugar

CHOCOLATE CHIP COOKIES

RECIPE BY PIPER BENJAMIN

There are two kinds of chocolate chip cookie fans out there: the hard, thinner, crunchy chocolate chip folks and the softer, gooey, fluffy, cake-like scrumptious fans. I prefer the latter. Gimme gooey every day! My daughter, Piper, made this riff off of the famous Levain Bakery cookies, which are so popular in New York City. They are amazing and quickly became a fan favorite. I prefer them warm, so don't be afraid to eat them soon after baking or feel free to throw in the microwave for 10 seconds as well! These cookies can almost make you forget about barbecue.

Preheat the oven to 410°F (210°C, or gas mark 6). That's right. 410°F (210°C). Line two half-sheet pans with parchment paper.

In a stand mixer fitted with the paddle attachment, combine the butter chunks, brown sugar, good old-fashioned regular sugar, and eggs. Beat until the sugar dissolves and the butter is creamy, about 3 minutes.

In a separate bowl, mix the flour, cornstarch, salt, and baking soda. Whisk by hand until nice and dispersed throughout. Add all of the flour mix to the butter mixture and fold in by hand with a large spatula until it all comes together, about another minute or so. Don't overwork it! Gently fold in the chocolate chips.

Using a 2-ounce (60 ml) scoop or a ¼-cup (60 ml) measuring cup, portion the dough onto the prepared baking sheets, making sure not to put these guys too close together. Bake the sheets one at a time on the lower oven rack for exactly 6 minutes. Rotate the pan and bake on the upper rack for 3 or 4 more minutes, just until the edges are light brown.

Let the cookies rest on the baking sheet for 5 minutes and then transfer to cooling racks. Try to keep your friends and family away long enough to let them cool, but please note these are amazing while still warm.

Makes 18 big Chocolate Chip Cookies

- 1 cup (2 sticks, or 225 g) unsalted butter, diced and chilled
- 1 cup (225 g) packed light brown sugar
- ½ cup (100 g) granulated sugar
- 2 large eggs
- 2 ½ cups (312 g) all-purpose flour
- ¼ cup (130 g) cornstarch
- 1 teaspoon kosher salt
- ¾ teaspoon baking soda
- 2 cups (350 g) semi-sweet chocolate chips

ABOUT THE AUTHOR

Mitch Benjamin, founder of the Meat Mitch Barbecue (team and brand), is the inventor of sauces and rubs that are consistently among the most award-winning and decorated in the country. The Meat Mitch competition team has won the prestigious American Royal BBQ Sauce World Championship Competition and The Memphis in May World Championship BBQ Sauce Competition, and finished with a 1st, 2nd, and 3rd in the heralded National Barbecue and Grilling Competition. Meat Mitch products can be found in stores and national chains throughout the United States and in more than a dozen countries around the world.

In Kansas City, Mitch was named the "Barbecue Ambassador" to the city by none other than Legendary Hall-of-Fame baseball player, George Brett. Mitch has cooked for a variety of Major League Baseball festivities—even taking the field with a plate of ribs for the Home Run Derby Competition. In 2015, Mitch opened his first restaurant, Char Bar Smoked Meats and Amusements, in Kansas City. In a competitive BBQ environment, the restaurant won Best New Restaurant in Kansas City—all restaurants included, not just barbecue. In 2021, Mitch launches his newest restaurant, Meat Mitch Barbecue. Mitch has also cooked for the New York Yankees; has appeared on national television, including *Fox & Friends*, *Today*, and *Barstool Sports*; and consulted on Rosie's Smokehouse, a pioneering BBQ restaurant in Paris, France.

ACKNOWLEDGMENTS

In addition to everyone mentioned below, thanks to all my team members, plus all my amazing friends that pop in and out—too many to mention, but all loved.

THANKS TO THE MEAT MITCH TEAM

BRUCE TRECEK "The Cleaner," amongst many other colorful nicknames. Bruce has been there from the beginning and is the heart and soul of the team. He epitomizes Meat Mitch BBQ.

JAMIE BURRELL If the world had twelve Jamies, it would be a dozen times better! He is always there with a smile, willing to do anything to help the team and the first guy to hand you a beer. Where would I be without him?! We are so fortunate to have him.

CORY LAGERSTROM Corypedia, knows a little bit about everything. Plus he has extreme passion, is hardworking, and keeps us organized. Cory is the glue, and he keeps us pushing forward!

JIM MCCLYMONT If it starts to rain, Jim stands up, the clouds part, and the sun starts to shine.

DAN GILLHAM Gilly elevates every event to the next level when he arrives . . . level of what, we never know.

BILL JACKOBOICE Billy Jack . . . yup, that sums it up.

THANKS ALSO TO

CARY TAYLOR This book doesn't exist without Cary. He helped me in every aspect imaginable and is a Pro's Pro.

JULIA HABERER Brilliant mentor and teacher to my daughter, Piper. Instrumental with this book and everything we do.

ISAAC ALONGI Amazing photographer with a great appreciation for good food!

JILL JACKOBOICE Beacon of light, wisdom, and beauty. Her wit is all over the Meat Mitch brand.

GEORGE BRETT Amazing friend and mentor who opened so many doors in my life. Thank God he could hit a curveball.

LOUIS AND MELISSA KHENANE Extremely appreciative for the opportunity you provided to me to come to Paris, and for taking me in. Here's to your continued success!

TOMMY CLEMENTE He's there to help me before I even realize I need help. Thank you for everything.

NICK REDDELL Stud, thanks for all your help and support. Check out socialsmokersbbq.com.

CHAR BAR TEAM Thank you for all your support and partnership. This is a world-class team. Thanks especially to Mark Kelpe, James Westphal, Michael Peterson, and Jeremy Tawney.

JEFF DAVENPORT Thank you for all the opportunities you have given us with the Kansas City Royals and MLB.

THOM O'HEARN First-class editor that held my hand and got this book to the finish line. Thanks also to the rest of the Quarto team!

TRINA KAHLE Food stylist extraordinaire—she honestly turns her apron into a cape and flies around a kitchen.

MICHELLE TWIBELL Runs Meat Mitch and ¾ of my life. Yes, she is a saint.

SCOTT REDLER Absurdly successful mentor and partner (founder of Freddy's Frozen Custard & Steakburgers) who I look forward to working with for many years in the restaurant business in our new Meat Mitch Barbecue restaurant venture.

JIM HICKEY The Father of my smoke.

JERRY KNEAREM American Royal Legend and everyone's "best guy I ever met."

ROD GRAY One of the best pitmasters in the world and great mentor to me.

JEFF STEHNEY Founder of Joe's Kansas City and the first person to give my sauce a chance and put it on his shelf. A BBQ icon and Hall-of-Famer.

RESOURCES

THE BIG ONES

MEAT MITCH (MEATMITCH.COM)

Of course you gotta' check this one out. My website is the place to buy all my sauces, rubs, and smoked meats online. While you are there, click around to find out about any news, watch videos, and explore the brand!

CHAR BAR (CHARBARKC.COM)

See what we're up to at the restaurant. And of course, stop on by when you're in KC!

KANSAS CITY CATTLE COMPANY (KCCATTLECOMPANY.COM)

This was our host for all those beautiful BBQ shots on the farm. The company was founded in 2016 by owner Patrick Montgomery, grounded upon the experiences of Patrick during his time in the military (1st Ranger Battalion) combined with the hard lessons learned through sweat and blood to create respectable practices in agriculture. This is a veteran-owned and -operated company that prides itself on raising superior quality Wagyu beef for the same people and communities they once served. Since Kansas City Cattle Company's beginnings in 2016, the growth and support received from across the United States has afforded Patrick the opportunity to hire more veterans and become one of the leading purveyors of Wagyu beef. From being selected and voted on as having the World's Best Hot Dog in 2019, to establishing a customer base and shipping Wagyu beef to all 50 states, Kansas City Cattle Company continues to carry on the mission year after year.

BARON SPICES & SEASONINGS (BARONSPICES.COM)

Meat Mitch's copacker for spices.

GARDEN COMPLEMENTS (GARDENCOMPLEMENTS.COM)

Meat Mitch's copacker for sauce.

HARP BARBECUE (FACEBOOK.COM/HARPBARBECUE)

Thank you for your help with the amazing boudin.

FEATURED, MENTIONED, OR OTHERWISE WORTH CHECKING OUT

AMERICAN BBQ SYSTEMS
americanbarbecuesystems.com

AMERICAN ROYAL BBQ americanroyal.com/bbq

AU CHEVAL auchevaldiner.com

BARON OF BBQ PAUL KIRK baron-of-bbq.com

BARSTOOL SPORTS barstoolsports.com

BIG POPPA SMOKERS bigpoppasmokers.com

BUD & ALLEY'S WATERFRONT RESTAURANT
budandalleys.com

BUTCHER BBQ butcherbbq.com

CHIGGER CREEK WOOD PRODUCTS chiggercreek.com

COCHON BUTCHER cochonbutcher.com

ENRIQUETA'S SANDWICH SHOP enriquetas.com

GENO'S STEAKS genosteaks.com

HABBERSETT SCRAPPLE habbersettscrapple.com

HARDCORE CARNIVORE hardcorecarnivore.com

JACCARD CORPORATION jaccard.com

JOE'S KANSAS CITY BAR-B-QUE joeskc.com

KANSAS CITY BARBECUE SOCIETY kcbs.us

KOSMO'S Q kosmosq.com

KURLBAUM FARMS kurlbaumtomatoes.com

memphisbbqnetwork.com

MEAT CHURCH meatchurch.com

MEMPHIS IN MAY memphisinmay.org

MILI VILLAMIL PHOTOGRAPHY milivillamil.com

MOMOFUKU momofuku.com

OKLAHOMA JOE'S oklahomajoes.com

PAT'S KING OF STEAKS patskingofsteaks.com

ROSIE'S SMOKEHOUSE rosies-smokehouse.eatbu.com

ROYAL OAK royaloak.com

SHUN CUTLERY shun.kaiusa.com

SMOKING GUN PRO® HANDHELD COCKTAIL SMOKER

STUBB'S BBQ stubbsaustin.com

THERMOWORKS thermoworks.com

TRAEGER GRILLS traegergrills.com

UBONS BARBEQUE ubonsbbq.com

VICTORINOX swissarmy.com/us/en

WEBER weber.com

YETI yeti.com

INDEX